# RV

# CAMPING

## IN NATIONAL PARKS

A Complete Guide
to the Best Road Trips in USA

DAMIEN TAYLOR

# Table of Contents

# Introduction

RV camping is one of the most enjoyable ways to pass the time on long road trips. You can go on adventures, have fun, and relax with a recreational vehicle. RV camping is among the nicest ways to have fun on a long road trip while still caring for your other necessities. It is the most cost-effective mode of transportation. Depending on the number of people in your traveling party, you can save up to 50 percent off lodging costs. RVs are more comfortable than tents, pop-up camps, and other modes of travel. RVs come in various forms and sizes and can be outfitted with amenities for a comfortable life on the road.

However, RV camping entails much more than packing your belongings and driving off to experience the great outdoors. The learning curve is fairly high when organizing an RV camping vacation. Many full-timers gain experience in pop-up campers and RV rentals before settling on a permanent camper for their travels. However, you are not required to pursue this path, even though it provides advantages.

After retirement, you can buy an RV, accept a mobile career, or spend more time with your loved ones. There is no better way to get closer as a group than by sharing the planning, execution, and enjoyment of the trip's meals, excursions, and activities.

This book guides you through everything for an enjoyable and safe RV trip. It covers everything about your RV, from the benefits of owning vs. renting to packing tips and maintenance procedures. You'll get useful hints for reducing stress when planning your excursions and taking your first RV road trip.

This book goes into great detail on everything. It is better than other books because of its simplicity and hands-on approach.

It is advised to pay special attention to safety recommendations and packing basics since they are meant for your protection. Remember, safeguarding your conveniences, connections, and camper is as crucial as preparing for comfort. This book includes several suggestions and tactics for cutting costs while ensuring pleasure, comfort, and safety. Mistakes are unavoidable, but learning to prevent and manage them can help lessen their effect and decrease the likelihood of accidents, theft, and other problems.

Most campsites and RV parks have facilities to accommodate various campers. However, it's wise to bring extra supplies just in case. Whether you're taking your RV on the road for a family vacation, a school break, a sabbatical, or as your primary residence, knowing what to anticipate helps you and your loved ones stay safe.

Don't hesitate to keep reading if you want to get your hands on these helpful hints and be well-prepared for RV camping.

# Chapter 1

# Planning and Budgeting

▆▆▆▆▆▆▆▆▆▆▆▆▆▆▆

Planning and budgeting are indispensable tools in nearly all endeavors and situations and are more prevalent in business settings. These analytical tools can be used when preparing for your impending trip.

They assist in setting seemingly impossible goals and developing a budget. This approach is used in companies to help management assess various options and establish financial benchmarks by recalculating and re-estimating costs, shifting target dates, and reevaluating goals. These aspects are feasible due to planning and budgeting.

This chapter is divided into two sections to discuss budgeting and planning effectively.

## Budgeting

Realizing the expenses for inside and outside of your RV helps you anticipate whether or not you will have enough money to meet your needs and satisfy your wants.

Four main advantages to RV travel are:

- Not paying for a hotel room to sleep in
- Not paying for transportation to and from wherever you wish to go
- Having a kitchen close by so that hunger is never an issue
- Seeing most of the attractions (the reason you wanted to go camping in the first place) without walking all day or sharing a tour vehicle.

## Which National Park to Visit First and Why

Due to the size and diversity of the United States, there are numerous national parks to visit. However, it is difficult to decide which park to visit first, despite its importance.

So, what are the important factors to consider?

### Bookings

The adage "the early bird gets the worm" holds true in this situation. You shouldn't be surprised that many people have the same travel plans as you and want to go simultaneously. Hence, you must make your reservation as early as possible, even a week before you leave for your trip.

Several national parks in the United States provide camping areas for RVs; however, you must make a reservation to secure a spot and do so promptly if you want to reserve a suitable spot at an affordable price. This is important if you plan to travel during peak season. These campgrounds offer various hookups and conveniences, so research, inquire, and confirm before embarking on your journey.

The average entrance fee to a national park is $35. You can pay the admission fee when making your reservation if you only intend to visit one or two parks. However, if you intend to visit more national parks, you'll save money purchasing an America the Beautiful Pass.

### Seasons

The season you travel in (summer, winter, or fall) impacts your budget significantly. For example, the cost of medications you might need to treat a cold should be factored into your travel budget if you're going during the winter.

Additionally, blankets and sweatshirts would occupy most of your storage space. If you're traveling during the holiday season, be prepared to spend more because it is more challenging to make reservations, and camping costs are higher.

Fall is usually the best time to go camping, as the weather is pleasant for lounging, and almost everything goes on sale. If traveling to a region with extreme temperatures, allocate some of your RV's budget toward new purchases.

### Gas

Gas is one of the most important considerations for your RV camping trip. Calculate how much gas you'll use so that you don't find yourself in a bind running out of gas and can't afford to replace it. It will be an awful situation. Once you know how many miles you will travel, you can calculate how much gas you need.

To calculate the gas estimate, use Google Maps to estimate the total miles you will travel between your destinations. Add a few additional miles in case you go somewhere not originally planned. Divide the calculated total miles by the gas mileage of your RV.

Multiply the resulting value by the average gas price. For example, if you travel 2,000 miles at 25 miles per gallon and pay $4.00 per gallon for diesel, you should expect to spend approximately $320 on gas. Your actual costs will vary depending on how meticulously you plan.

To reduce your spending, research the differences in the gas prices between the states and strategize when to stop, like stopping in Nevada before entering California.

*Food*

Food is another essential factor to consider. Your sightseeing experience will not be enjoyable if you and your companions do not have enough food and water to last each day. Having enough money to buy food avoids the hassle of preparing most meals. Cooking your meals is an option if you want to save money.

You must know that dining out, even at local restaurants, will cost you approximately three times as much as if you prepared your food.

Plan how much money you need to buy food for meals and occasional splurges. After all, what's the point of going on a camping trip if you can't try the local cuisine?

Consider your daily expenses and multiply that by the number of days you plan to spend traveling.

There are ways to cut grocery costs.

### *Your Budget*

The money you have available for a travel camp determines where you will go first and, by extension, where you will go next (how far you are willing to travel).

If you're on a tight budget, you wouldn't travel too far, and you'd preferably start with the park closest to you.

Your budget is important because it ensures you do not overspend and can deal with emergencies like health and maintenance when they happen.

Getting a good night's sleep after the day's events is essential, and thanks to a good budget, you can.

### *Your Interest*

Each park has something unique (you will learn about them in later chapters), which explains why there are so many. Regardless of which state you choose to visit, a park that suits your interests awaits you. For instance, if you appreciate the beauty of nature's colors, you should visit Anza-Borrego Desert Park in California in the spring to see them in full bloom after the winter rains.

You have significantly more options if you are interested in culture, arts, and history. You can visit the First Ladies National Historical Park in Ohio or the African American Civil War Memorial in Washington, D.C.

Fall is the best time to travel because it has fewer tourists than summer, more festival excitement, clearer weather than winter, and cheaper accommodations. However, fall is not the best option if you want to go skiing or fishing.

## Do Seasons Have an Impact on Road Trips?

You wake up one morning during the winter and look outside, thinking, "When it's summer, I'm going to the beach and getting my skin tanned. Oh, I simply cannot wait." You've just planned your leisure time based on the seasons. However, be aware that road trips are affected by seasons caused by atmospheric factors, such as temperature, sunshine, wind velocity, and precipitation. Numerous individuals are mindful of these elements and how they affect travel satisfaction.

Travel satisfaction is the feeling you get from evaluating your daily travel conditions. Many travelers derive more satisfaction from slow modes of transportation, like cycling and walking than from cars due to access, the risk of slow traffic, the inability to choose which lane and speed to use, and the likelihood of being irritated by other road users.

Good weather conditions can make your time spent in your RV enjoyable. In contrast, bad weather can ruin your entire vacation by placing you in congested areas, requiring you to reschedule or cancel your trip, or causing you to suffer and become ill. The weather could interfere with your internet connection, leaving you stranded at a location for hours if no one is around to ask for directions or help.

Before your trip, check for extremely high or low temperatures and heavy precipitation (rain or snow), as these greatly impact travel satisfaction more than light winds. When planning your trip, consider the weather forecast for the days you are traveling, so if you are forced to endure inclement weather, you will be prepared.

## Planning

Generally, planning saves time, money, and stress. To plan seasonally, you must consider where you'll be camping, the weather, and the season. Do you intend to go skiing? Then you must plan your travel for winter. In the summer, do you plan on visiting the beach? Do you intend to stay until the holiday season is over? If you put off making reservations for your preferred season for too long, you risk missing out on all the fun that could have been yours.

So, why is it important to plan according to the seasons?

### *Your Trip Does Not Disrupt Your Schedule*

Nobody enjoys going on vacation only to have to return home sooner than anticipated due to an issue they failed to consider. For this reason, planning is extremely important.

A vacation from work, perhaps over winter, should be taken in advance of the date set aside for your trip. Furthermore, be prepared to handle any eventuality, leaving the remaining problems as purely unavoidable surprises.

### *You Are Ready Beforehand*

Planning in advance and according to the seasons enables you to pack the necessities for your trip. You know to bring sweatshirts, heaters, socks, and head warmers if you're traveling in winter.

Pack light dresses, strapless tops, shorts, and tanning lotion if traveling during summer. So, if the forecaster has given you an idea of what the next two days will be like, you are well-prepared.

### *You've Already Scheduled Your Activities*

It is unreasonable to travel during summer with the intention of skiing. If you enjoy skiing or snowboarding, schedule your trip during winter. If you want to participate in treasure hunts, plan your trip for autumn. It might seem like something everyone should be aware of, but if you do not prepare for it, you will miss it.

Planning according to the seasons allows you to have the tools for these activities available, saving you the money you would have spent on renting if you hadn't planned ahead.

### *You Are Less Worried*

When you plan for the entire season at once, as opposed to planning each trip for a different season, you save time and reduce the likelihood of making careless mistakes like forgetting to bring necessary items and booking the same thing twice.

You can decide how one trip would lead to the next and make your travel plans accordingly (skiing on one trip could lead you to treasure hunting on another). If you take these steps, you can focus on having a good time instead of worrying about potential problems.

### *More Contentment*

You can make the most of your trips if you attend to camping essentials, including seasonal festivities. With the big stuff taken care of, you'll have more time to explore on your terms, especially if you've already done preliminary research into the seasonal wonders you might encounter.

## Types of Trips

There are numerous types of trips, but the following are the five most common:

1. Family Vacation

2. Solo Trips

3. National Park Trips

4. Road Trips

5. Business Trips

Perfect vacations are always the result of extensive planning and brainstorming, regardless of the destination. It's always fun to plan a trip on the spur of the moment based on your instincts until you have to decide on the most important details.

The first step in planning is to create a checklist with the associated costs. A well-organized checklist is essential, so you do not forget anything and can easily see everything you intend to bring.

Here are a few things to consider when planning your trip:

### Your Destination

Whether or not external factors like movies or books influence your choice of destination, you must consider your budget and the time of year you will be traveling.

Research the time of year optimal for visiting each place on your itinerary, the money required for each trip, and the accessibility.

### Your Reservations

Bookings are an essential part of nearly all vacation preparation aspects. Due to the seasonal nature of most rips, making reservations in advance will help you avoid incurring additional expenses when seasons are closed. You may stay in the park if you have enough money set aside (if it is allowed). Otherwise, finding a hotel near the park would be less expensive and more convenient.

### Your Duration of Stay

There is no ideal length of stay for a specific destination. You might become bored and decide to return early, or you enjoy yourself and extend your stay by one or two days.

It is prudent to account for both possibilities when planning to avoid confusion. This aspect of planning has the greatest impact on your budget. Your budget could stop or encourage you if you decide to stay for longer. Estimate the number of days you will stay and then create a budget for your food, transportation, lodging, and other incidentals.

### *Your Daily Activities*

This depends on your budget and the duration of your stay. If you strictly adhere to a to-do list, then sticking to this plan shouldn't be a problem. It's possible that a few things will change, but the essentials should remain the same.

Schedule no more than three activities a day if the trip's purpose is to relax and have fun. Before you embark on your trip, confirm the availability of desired activities at your destination(s).

### *Review Your Plan*

It is not sufficient to simply plan; you must review your plan to ensure you have not omitted crucial elements. Changes in the weather are highly unpredictable, as can the spread of festivals and sociopolitical scenarios.

Therefore, researching your trip is an important part of the planning process. Examine your checklist and budget, eliminate anything unnecessary, and mark off what has been sorted.

## Packing for Your Trip

Many people learn the hard way that packing isn't as easy as they thought after they've traveled quite a distance and realize they've forgotten something crucial. If you forget an essential item, you will be disappointed.

The subsequent frantic searching and scrambling to locate the closest store can cause anxiety. Overpacking guarantees you'll spend the rest of your trip scrambling to find everything. Not only will you have to pay extra to check your bags when flying, but you'll also have to lug around excessive stuff.

So, what should you pack? You should pack only enough items for the number of days you will be away from home, including food, over-the-counter medicines, water, and sources of entertainment.

Start with small bags and cover RV compartments you do not intend to fill to avoid carrying too many items. After packing the essentials, a second tip is to carefully consider every item you intend to bring.

## Essentials for a Road Trip

Regardless of the journey's duration, you must bring these essential items; food, clothing, car chargers, and snacks (fresh fruits, fresh vegetables like carrots, and mixed nuts). Also, a physical map (if you can get one and are unfamiliar with the area), a cooler, a cozy blanket, a microwave, battery fans, car batteries, an A/C inverter, tire inflators, touch lights, water bottles, headphones, napkins, lotions, tissues, soaps, shoes and slippers, travel pillows, utensils, and nylon bags are essential.

Don't forget to take extra clothing items like shirts, sweatshirts, and jeans; you'll be glad you did. Items like sunscreen and mosquito repellents should not be forgotten.

Essentials for your stay must always come first when packing for a trip, followed by other less important items. Food, clothing, and water should be top of your list. Fashion items like additional shoes, necklaces, tote bags, and sunglasses can be included. Books, Bluetooth speakers, and periodicals are easy to transport and necessary for a day at the beach.

### What Not to Carry

- Expensive and valuable items.

- Original copies of important documents and photographs.

- Flammable liquids.

Traveling can be stressful, particularly in planning and budgeting. When we visit new places, we usually like to purchase a memento as proof that we were there and as a means of remembrance. However, don't feel obligated to buy anything if you can't afford it. Upon arrival at any destination, be certain to acquire a map. They are free, can be used as souvenirs, contain information on the must-see attractions and trailheads, and will help you find your way if you become lost.

Reading about your destination before you travel helps you prepare for the weather and activities, like biking or skiing, that you might engage in. If you do not have the necessary equipment for your planned activities, you must include rental fees in your budget (purchase these items away from your camping destination to save money). Reading about your destination will assist in gathering information on booking and when the National Park offers free admission. Many National Parks offer free admission days, which will help you save money.

For ease of comfort and assurance while on your road trip, it is always best to be prepared for unfortunate events. Injuries, allergies, wounds, or illnesses can occur when least expected. Hospitalization could be a possibility and very expensive if you don't have insurance. Allocating for this occurrence in your budget is advisable.

To avoid offending the locals or getting into trouble, it's a good idea to familiarize yourself with the cultural norms of your travel destination. The activities you intend to do while camping impact your plan; hence, your budget has a greater impact. As a result, you must plan and budget carefully.

# Chapter 2

## Packing and Road Safety

An RV camping trip is the ideal outing or activity for the holidays, whether in winter or summer. The National Parks Service reports 327 million leisure visits to the nation's parks, demonstrating that national parks are popular tourist destinations.

Whether it's your first time or not, the beauty and scenery of a road trip are unparalleled. It's an opportunity to unwind, explore, and enjoy nature. It provides a once-in-a-lifetime experience, but a lack of planning, emergencies, unsafe travel, or vehicle trouble can dampen the excitement.

A road trip requires adequate preparations, planning, packing, and, most importantly, road safety. There are suggestions, checklists, and essentials to pack for a fun-filled road trip. This chapter discusses and informs you about two aspects of road trip preparation: packing and road safety.

## Packing

Packing for a road trip is not difficult, but it can be overwhelming. An RV camping trip is exciting, but packing the right equipment can be stressful. You must account for feeding, weather, and accessories while not forgetting the necessities. Without proper planning, you might have luggage full of unnecessary items. In contrast, with appropriate planning, you will have a compact backpack or luggage with the right amount of items without getting a headache. So, how do you plan a road trip?

Preparing for a road trip begins with planning the duration, routes, destinations, and sights to see along the way and allowing time to visit unexpected areas of interest.

The length of the trip influences your packing and camping arrangements. A small backpack and a few clothes will suffice for a short trip, but a larger pack will be required for a longer trip. The length of your journey will impact your feeding, clothing, and health arrangements significantly.

If you know how long you'll be gone, you can choose your food, snacks, and treats wisely. Some foods cannot withstand a lot of heat or moisture; planning the duration of the trip indicates what food to avoid, what to bring along, and how to package them to prevent waste and unnecessary spending.

Weather forecasting is another advantage of planning ahead. Knowing the routes you'll take, how long you'll be gone, and the area's weather patterns will help you prepare well. The expected weather conditions during the trip will affect your camping arrangements. So, this knowledge allows you to pack the necessary items to protect yourself from harsh conditions and deal with emergencies.

Packing for an RV camping trip does not have to be a stressful experience. Your arrangements will be guided if you take the right steps and practice the simple but fundamental tips. Begin by obtaining a detailed map of the area's sights, sounds, and routes. Getting a map emphasizes the importance of planning ahead.

Using a map, whether online or on paper, you can determine how to get to your destination on time, mark routes and places you want to see, and access routes to the park timeously. It also helps you avoid roads that aren't in good condition, are blocked by traffic, or have heavy traffic activity. You can mark RV parks or hotels for your stay, determine whether your vehicle is permitted at certain parks, locate gasoline stations, compare gas prices, and plan your trip budget.

The next step is to pack effectively. Packing mistakes can quickly deflate a road trip's energy and enthusiasm. While you want to enjoy the comfort and freedom of a classic RV trip, you don't want to overload your luggage. When packing for a road trip, only bring what you need. Categorize your item list so that you pack the necessary items, leaving room for other items. In essence, make a priority scale, categorize your options, and choose what is most needed.

The mode of transportation for the road trip influences how much you pack, and using an RV means you might have limited space. It is recommended to pack compactly to avoid overloading the RV and make full use of the available space.

Here are a few pointers to help you organize and categorize your packing for a healthy and hearty adventure:

### *Documents*

After you've planned your trip, ensure to pack your documents and other identification or important information. You might not see the need for these at first, but this information could be required at checkpoints, parks, or entrances.

The most important documentation you need on the road includes your driver's license, vehicle or RV registration, RV manual, campground reservations, and relevant medical information. Your roadside assistance information, passport (if traveling between countries), camping checklists, and RV maintenance history are useful. Remember, keep them away from moisture and extreme temperatures, and use a waterproof folder to keep them safe.

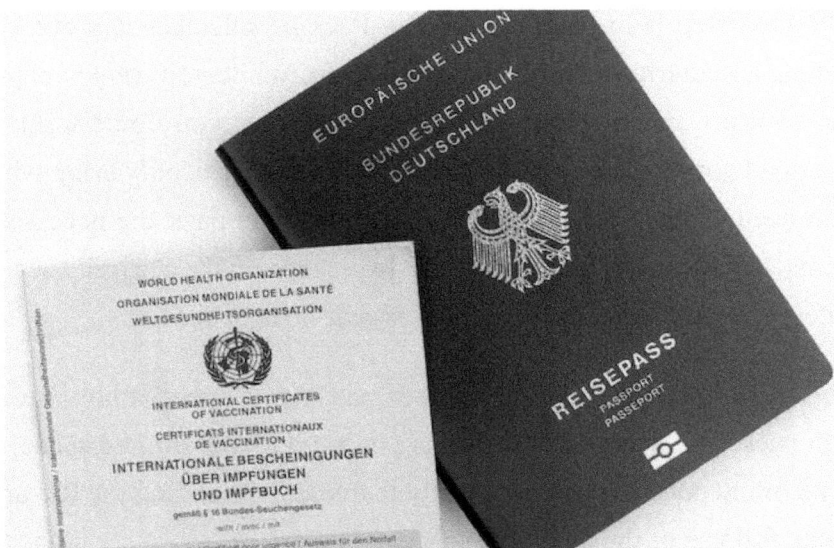

### *Health and Hygiene*

Health and hygiene cannot be compromised on a road trip. A minor headache that worsens, an infected injury or bruise, or an infection from a poisonous plant or thorn can end the trip or dampen the mood - making adequate preparations for your and others' health and hygiene while traveling is critical.

Your first aid kit should be the first thing that comes to mind regarding health. Always have a good first aid kit for camping trips. It should include bandages, ointments, methylated spirits, scissors, sanitizers, antiseptics, and other items useful in an emergency or when basic care is required.

Additionally, packing painkillers, a thermometer, cough syrup, prescription and allergy drugs, sunscreen, and antibiotics is advisable. You can buy a first aid kit from a store if you cannot put one together. Please keep it in a location accessible to friends and family but out of reach to children.

Hygiene is also crucial. Bring multipurpose shampoos, toiletries, and soaps to conserve space and money. Make sure your hygiene supplies are as unscented and simple as possible; pack wipes and use waterproof bags.

### *Clothing and Comfort*

Your clothing selection will affect the comfort of the road or camping trip. So, imagine the weather and temperature conditions before packing your wearables.

First, consider the weather and activities you intend to undertake during your trip. Bring long, thick socks, warm jackets, hats, gloves, and sweaters if you're going somewhere cold. It will immediately simplify your clothing options and assist you in selecting the most comfortable clothing. Extra blankets and long pants or underwear are also useful.

If you're camping and expect rain, a raincoat, boots, umbrellas, and other appropriate rain gear will come in handy. A few rags and extra pieces of clothing will suffice if it gets muddy. Portable fans and sun blockers will keep the RV cool in hot weather, while sunglasses, sun hats, umbrellas, and light blankets keep you safe and comfortable during hot nights.

Shower and hand towels, pillows, bedding sheets, and pillowcases should be packed for your comfort. Don't bring too many comfort items to avoid crowding the space; bring just enough to ensure everyone's happiness.

### *Kitchen Essentials*

You never know how much is too much with food during a road trip, so when packing food, consider the length of the trip, the number of people traveling, the type of food, food markets or supermarkets along your route, and the storage and kitchen amenities available.

Planning your meals for the trip will make feeding arrangements easier. Keep perishable foods fresh with a couple of coolers and ice, and keep spillable liquids in containers to avoid a mess. Reusable tableware and plastic bags are environmentally friendly options and bring clean-up items to keep the area hygienically neat after eating.

A camp stove, Dutch oven, or griddle will suffice if you intend to cook outside. Packing light kitchenware will make the trip less difficult. A few pots and pans will do, while snacks, appetizers, and treats will keep the kids entertained.

### *Electronics and Entertainment*

You'll need some connection to the outside world and entertainment to keep everyone engaged while on an RV trip.

Get a voltmeter to check battery power, a digital line monitor to monitor generator frequency, AC voltage, and bad wiring, and an electrical adapter to charge your devices. Simultaneously, hunt for information on fuses in your RV manual. Bring lanterns, flashlights, and rechargeable headlamps on your trip. Don't forget to bring the required power cords.

There are numerous options for indoor and outdoor entertainment. For indoor activities, bring board games, coloring pages for children and adults, a deck of cards, and books. Bring sports equipment like Frisbees, volleyball nets, squirt guns, and comfy camp chairs for outdoor activities, on your buying list, including headphones, a portable stereo, phones, computers, and a Wi-Fi connection.

### Camping Gear

Since this is a camping trip, you must plan your sleeping and camping arrangements. You'll probably sleep in your RV if you're traveling with one, but most RVers pitch tents, so you might as well.

The number of people on your trip determines the size of your camping equipment. If you're pitching a tent, you need sleeping bags, a tent, and a few accessories like flashlights and blankets. If you're going hiking, you'll need hiking boots, water bottles, a notepad, and a camera, if not your phone.

### Toolbox

An RV toolbox and emergency roadside kit are essential items to bring on a road trip for safety and emergency repairs. They have the tools and information to keep your RV running. A hammer, duct tape, screwdriver, jumper cables, sealant, tire pressure gauge, and roof patches are required.

Keep the RV toolbox out of reach of children; if you have an outdoor storage space, use it. Use sturdy, small, neatly arranged toolboxes for easy placement and weight distribution. Coolants and caustic fluids should be kept separate from other metals and in airtight containers.

Don't forget to bring plenty of fresh water; a couple of gallons or large water bottles will go a long way. If you're bringing children, remember to make arrangements for them. Take extra clothes and snacks, keep things organized, and closely monitor their movements. Take only people-friendly pets, and make arrangements for them. Bring treats, medications, and hygiene products to care for them.

### *Essentials*

Even with all the guidelines and tips, it is possible to forget to pack some essential items for an RV camping trip. Here's a list of critical things to pack in your luggage:

- Maps and documents.

- Emergency roadside kit.

- First aid kit.

- Jumper cables.

- Snacks.

- Water bottles.

- Camping gear.

- Plastic wraps and bags.

- Waterproof bags.

- Disinfectants and wipes.

- Cooler.

- Canned foods.

- Food staples.

- Extra cash.

- Rain gear.

- Socks.

- Deodorants and hygiene products.

- Lysol wipes.

- Games.

- Chargers.

There are many things to pack for a road trip, but knowing the length of the trip and the routes you'll take will help you decide what and how much to pack. Pack what you need, bring extra blankets and clothing, and keep your first aid kit nearby. Maintain a charged phone for communication and protect yourself and others on the trip.

## Road Safety

For a successful road trip, the safety of persons and property must be ensured. Due to blind spots, maintenance issues, and special considerations, driving and maintaining an RV differs from operating and maintaining a standard car.

Before you start your RV vacation, it's a good idea to examine the road conditions, traffic along the route, and the weather, and carry out regular maintenance before taking your RV on the road.

Correct maintenance includes checking the fluid levels and searching for leaks. Check the engine oil, coolant, brake fluid, and transmission oil levels before driving the RV. The water system should be cleaned, de-winterized, and checked for leaks, while the battery also needs inspection.

Additionally, you should turn on the engine and check the gauge readings and indicator functionality. Contact your mechanic if you detect anything out of the ordinary.

Check the humidity in the air vents, windows, and tire pressure while checking your safety equipment. Check all antennae and secure trash cans and access doors. Disconnect the antennae, steps, and slides, and secure any loose items within the RV.

Keep your luggage organized and compact, so you don't overburden the RV. Properly clean the RV, store your toolbox and luggage safely and securely, and drain and replenish the hoses. Check the automobile's mechanical components are in good working condition and that the vehicle is roadworthy to avoid problems at checkpoints and car problems on the road.

Below are additional things to observe to ensure proper road safety caution:

### Driving Safely

Driving safely is an important part of an RV camping trip, in addition to vehicle maintenance and ensuring the RV is roadworthy. Since an RV is larger and heavier than a regular car, you have less precision and control.

Although some people have a lot of experience driving an RV and how to drive one safely, we should never be too confident because accidents happen. When driving an RV, caution and patience are essential.

You should not overload the RV to ensure safety while driving. Every RV has a weight-carrying capacity, which should not be exceeded. This tip leads to more information on how to drive an RV safely. More information can be found in your RV manual.

Please be patient. Because it is a large vehicle, you must exercise caution when turning, overtaking, or crossing intersections. Most RVs have a higher-than-average speed limit, but that doesn't mean we should drive recklessly. Drive at a leisurely pace and allow plenty of time to arrive at your destination so you don't have to rush.

Drive slowly and make slow turns to avoid overturning. Maintain a safe distance between yourself and other vehicles, navigate to the right whenever possible because it is usually free, and be alert. Since the RV has many blind spots, make wide turns, and indicate early before turning.

Break early; don't slam on the brakes as you would with a smaller car; doing so with an RV could be disastrous. The weight of the RV adds to the rig, making slowing down and speeding up different than a car, so plan your activities ahead of time.

Use runway ramps if you can't stop or slow down. Braking is slow, so if you feel out of control, proceed to nearby runway ramps while signaling to other vehicles for space and alertness.

These ramps were created to help out-of-control trucks and RVs. Maintain control of the ramp by cutting the wheels in one direction, steadying the RV, and engaging the brake.

Drive during the day and avoid driving in bad weather. Fatal road accidents occur at night, so move during the day to accommodate the length and weight of the RV. Before you hit the road, check the weather forecast. Any condition that would disrupt your driving experience or reduce your visibility should be avoided.

Driving an RV implies you are aware that your plans are subject to change. If the weather isn't cooperating, make another plan and be prepared to adapt to changing conditions. For safe travel, use GPS or a trip planner. You'll find points of interest and campgrounds at your leisure, and always take the safest and quickest routes.

As a driver, you are responsible for everyone in the RV. Keep your eyes on the road and avoid engaging in any non-driving activity that will distract you. Do not drive if there are strong winds or if you are distracted. Importantly, take time to rest if you're tired.

Adjust your mirrors to help you as much as possible while driving; it will also keep you calm during trailer sway. Trailer sway occurs when a trailer becomes entangled in the slipstream of a nearby vehicle or is hit by side winds. The aerodynamics of an RV cause it to sway back and forth; remain calm and minimize this effect. Set the wheel straight, take your foot off the gas, and brake rather than accelerate to regain control.

Remember to accept assistance when parking; this simple tip is frequently overlooked. It's difficult to park an RV, the mirrors don't provide a clear view, and tail swings must be avoided. Seek assistance from an observer, security personnel, or a passenger to avoid hitting something or someone in your blind spot. Lower the windows to receive instructions, have the person helping you stand close to you, and carefully maneuver the vehicle until it is parked. Driving and parking an RV becomes easier with practice.

When driving an RV, check the mechanical and non-mechanical parts of the vehicle. Repair leaks, correctly gauge and pump tires, disconnect antennas, close windows, and secure important documents and large items.

Drive with caution and patience, maintain a safe distance between yourself and other vehicles, adhere to speed limits, and maintain focus. Don't overload the vehicle. Keep everything inside the RV clean to prevent the spread of germs, take wider turns, and accept assistance as needed. Maintain your focus and avoid driving while impaired.

RV camping trips combine fun, adventure, and exploration, but improper planning and road safety can cancel or disrupt the trip. Plan your trip ahead of time so that you are aware of the weather, duration, activities, and luggage size. Ensure to bring only the necessities. Organize and arrange your items as needed, keeping things compact, clean, and clutter-free.

Double-check your items and leave room for miscellaneous and extras. Keep your toolbox, roadside kit, and first aid kit close at hand but out of reach of children. Use small boxes to distribute weight, and plan ahead for bringing children or pets.

Packing and road safety is critical to the road trip, and maintaining the utmost safety while packing essential items will ensure you have a comfortable and blissful outing. Maintain your RV properly, and use trip planning apps or GPS for ease of movement. Avoid driving in bad weather or at night, make no rash decisions, and go slowly. Get assistance in overcoming blind spots, avoiding distractions, and traveling safely.

# Chapter 3

# Arizona State Parks

The diverse region of Arizona State attracts the attention of millions of visitors every year. Arizona State is a must-visit location on every traveler's list, home to the Grand Canyon, several national monuments, wildlife parks, beautiful lakes, and stunning state parks. One of the best ways to experience Arizona's natural beauty is by RV camping, and what better way to do that than in the various state parks in Arizona? If you're a fan of open spaces, windswept lakes, beautiful mountains, or gorgeous deserts, the diverse Arizona State Parks will be perfect for satisfying your inner adventurer.

RV camping is a time-honored tradition of America, filled with deep-rooted memories of childhood, family, and adventure. No matter what season you decide to travel, Arizona state parks will provide the best atmosphere you can hope to have on your camping trip. Since Arizona is home to some of the finest state parks in the country, there's no shortage of pristine scenery, exquisite wilderness, and a sense of mystery in each state park. Whether you're traveling alone, with your family, friends, or romantic partner, there are state parks suitable for everyone catering to your every need.

There are 15 parks in the state, many providing developed campsites, picnicking facilities, water supply, and electric hookups. Regardless of your RV's size, you can find a camping site perfect for your needs. Arizona has no shortage of breathtaking places to stay, so take your pick from the variety of options available. However, keep in mind that not all of Arizona's parks are RV-friendly. There's nothing wrong with parking at a private campground, but it doesn't provide the same level of convenience and comfort experienced when camping at a state park. So, it's better to research prior to your trip and select a state park that matches all your needs.

This chapter highlights some of the most popular state parks in Arizona, which are RV-friendly and offer a number of activities to make your trip perfect.

## Patagonia Lake State Park

Patagonia Lake State Park, established in 1975, is located in southeastern Arizona among beautiful rolling hills and mountains. The park offers a fully functional campground, a stunning beach, picnic areas, grills, tables, boats, walking trails, and a marina. If you're a fan of wildlife excursions, this state park has many opportunities to sight the great blue herons walking along the beach or the beautiful white deer wandering the hills.

Moreover, a lakeside market nearby offers all boating supplies and rentals for you to enjoy the water activities. If you're a fishing enthusiast, you'll be happy to know you can catch catfish, trout, bluegill, bass, and crappie varieties. The park is a popular fishing site for many visitors. Other activities include camping, hiking, picnicking, and water skiing. Additionally, guided bird walks, first-day hikes, and exhilarating boat tours for you to participate in are offered.

For history enthusiasts, Patagonia Lake State Park offers a fascinating historical overview of the park's original establishment. There are remnants of old New Mexico/Arizona railroad tracks showcased at the Nature Conservancy in Patagonia. The boat tours also provide an extensive overview of the history and vegetation of the surrounding area.

There is no better camping experience than at Patagonia Lake State Park. The lakeside camping at Patagonia ensures a fun and exhilarating experience, or a more relaxed one if you prefer. Essentially, your stay can be personalized according to your needs. The park has 105 developed campsites with 30 to 50-amp electric hook-ups that can be reserved. Each campsite has a fire ring, a picnic table, and a grill. Guidelines are given to ensure proper order. These include:

- Campsite reservations must be made prior to your visit. Reservations can be made online or by calling. Sites fill up quickly between May and November, so make a reservation as early as possible.

- Most campsite lengths vary, so there are no restrictions to the length of your RV. However, when making a reservation, ensure you reserve a spot that can accommodate your vehicle.

- Quiet hours must be observed from 9 PM to 8 AM. No loud music, voices, or noise from generators is permitted.

- No dogs or pets are permitted at the beach area. They can be kept in the west dry area.

- Jet skis and jet boats are prohibited on the lake. Additional watercraft rules must be followed.

- Moving or removing natural vegetation and rocks from the park premises is not permitted.

## Kartchner Caverns State Park

This state park is fascinating for explorers and history enthusiasts as it contains a rich history and interesting geological features. In 1974, two Arizona explorers set out to look for a cave no one had ever found before, and by some miracle, they found it. They kept the cave a secret before informing the property owners, the Kartchners, in 1978 about the cave. The story of Kartchner Caverns State Park is centered around this cave and its incredible exploration and development.

The Kartchner Caverns constitute about 2.5 miles of untouched cave passages with two featured rooms for tourists and visitors. These rooms are home to centuries-old limestone foundations. These cave passages are interesting for many visitors and are considered the main highlight of the state park. The programs and events at this particular state park are filled with educational tours and interesting activities.

Main events include a first-day hike along the foothills loop trails and a sunset hike along the same path. Kids can participate in the junior ranger experience. Other events include nature hikes, nightlife excursions, educational talks, and interactive sessions. There are countless opportunities to take a half or full-day side trip and explore the surrounding area. For instance, you could visit the city of Sierra Vista, experience a historical adventure by stopping at Tombstone Courthouse, or tour the scenic hideaway at Cochise Stronghold.

Once you've explored the park and surrounding regions, you can camp in the fully operating campgrounds near the caverns. It's the best place to get a good rest and wake up refreshed to explore. The campground has an adequate number of campsites for your RV. Each campsite has a table, hose bib, and power post. The electric hook-ups vary from 30 to 50 amp connections. The campsites' sizes vary from 30 inches to 60 inches accommodations, and pullout units are permitted. The showers and restroom facilities are located at the upper west side of the campground and have a 24/7 water supply. Campground guidelines include:

- Campsite reservations can be made online during the summer months. From June to October, reservations are first-come, first-served accommodations.

- The park has a 14-day stay limit for RV campers and other visitors.

- You must make reservations for programs or events you want to participate in, including cave tours.

- Ensure you have a paid camping permit to use the various campground facilities, including water and electric hookups and the dump station.

- Feeding birds or wildlife is strictly prohibited in the park grounds.

- No pets are permitted during the cave tours.

- Taking photos or videos is prohibited inside the caves

## Lyman Lake State Park

Originally an irrigation reservoir, Lyman Lake State Park encompasses a huge 1500-acre reservoir by the Colorado River. It is connected with Escudilla Mountain and Mount Baldy, where the water is channeled into this river valley. This lake is one of the rare water bodies in the northern part of Arizona that doesn't have boating restrictions. However, the west end of the lake is restricted, which isn't necessarily bad. The non-proximity of water skiers and speed boats gives fishermen a higher chance of catching various fish species, including largemouth bass, walleye, and catfish varieties.

The rest of the lake is open for the general public to participate in various water sports. Spring, fall, and summer are the peak seasons to visit this state park, with perfectly pleasant temperatures and a beautiful environment. Water activities include swimming, boating, fishing, and water skiing. Other programs include the first-day hike with a guided tour of the petroglyph trail. Additionally, many community events are arranged throughout the year, including Easter events, Christmas programs, and other holiday fun.

The camping experience at Lyman Lake State Park offers visitors a look at the wild side of Arizona's backcountry. The large campground offers a combination of adventure and relaxation for a perfect trip. Amenities include showers, restrooms, picnic tables, grills, fire rings, and electric and water hookups. A dump station is available for RV campers. There are a total of 56 campsites, with 38 of them containing hook-ups. Guidelines include:

- It is advised not to drink the lake water and instead opt for water available at water filters.

- Reservation and non-reservation sites are available and can be selected depending on your preference.

- Always keep your vehicle on established roads and within the defined speed limits.

- Pets are permitted but must be kept on a leash and picked up after.

- Wood gathering is strictly prohibited; fires can only be started in fire rings or grills.

- It is strictly prohibited to touch, move, or take any animals, plants, archeological or historical objects.

- Quiet hours are between 10 PM to 7 AM. No loud music or voices are allowed during this time.

## Dead Horse Ranch State Park

The unique name of this state farm has a simple backstory connected to it. In the late 1940s, the Ireys family came to Arizona to purchase a ranch. At one ranch they visited, they discovered a dead horse lying by the side of the road. After a few days of viewing different ranches, when the dad asked his kids which ranch they liked best, they replied, "the one with the dead horse" that name stuck even after the Arizona State Parks acquired this ranch.

This lovely state park is located in the River Valley Corridor of north central Arizona. In addition to access to spacious campgrounds, several other facilities are present at this state park. Walking trails, a playground, and the visitor center are the most popular places people like to explore. The place has a rustic atmosphere that goes perfectly with RV camping for the experience of a lifetime. Dead Horse Ranch State Park is a wonderful place to stay, especially if you're interested in learning the history and culture of this Arizona region. Ramadas and picnic areas can be reserved for daytime activities. Other activities include hiking, horseback riding, fishing, wildlife excursions, and educational programs.

The camping experience at Dead Horse Ranch State Park is one of a kind. More than 100 RV sites are available, with no RV length restrictions. So, whether you have a 40-foot motor home or a 65-foot trailer rig, you're welcome to stay at this park. In addition to electric and water hookups, restrooms, picnic tables, fire rings, and grills are provided for free. However, generators are prohibited. These camping guidelines must be followed:

- You can park a maximum of 2 vehicles per campsite, including your RV.

- All pets must be kept on a leash and cleaned up after. Pets are not permitted in park buildings.

- Firewood collecting is prohibited in the park. However, fires can be lit in the fire ring.

- Check-in time is 2 PM, and check-out time is 12 PM. Quiet hours must be observed between 10 PM and 8 AM.

- RV and vehicle washing is not permitted in the park.

- Swimming, wading, and boating are prohibited in the lagoons.

- Metal detecting or digging is not permitted in the park.

## Lake Havasu State Park

The lake Havasu shoreline is a sight to see. This beautiful state park is an ideal destination for your next RV camping trip, with its luxurious beaches, comfortable campsites, stunning nature trail, and functional boat ramps. Located near the London Bridge of Lake Havasu City, this spot has become a famous watersport location for many. The state park offers more than 50 campsites, a beautiful beach area, and a picnic shelter that can be reserved. Additionally, a large special events area is designated for birthdays, weddings, and special events, which can be reserved.

Numerous people visit the interpretive garden throughout the year, where they can observe the diverse wildlife in the park and desert. Desert cottontails, birds, and lizards are the most common animals observed on these nature trails. The state park campground offers a huge space open all year, making it the perfect camping stop during festivals and holidays while other parks are closed. Each site has access to electric and water hook-ups and a nearby dump station.

The best part? Your camping fees include all amenities, including electric and water hookups, showers and restrooms, and participation in park day activities. Camping guidelines include the following:

- The maximum length of stay is 14 days, with a limit of 6 guests per vehicle. The campsite has to be occupied overnight.

- Fires shouldn't be left unattended and be avoided in windy weather. Ensure you extinguish the fire completely before leaving the site.

- Amenities will only be provided to registered campers. Campsite reservations can be made beforehand or on arrival.

- Quiet hours must be observed from 10 PM to 6 AM, so ensure to turn off any loud music or generators for the night.

- Fireworks are strictly prohibited.

- RVs must only be parked in designated and paved areas.

## Lost Dutchman State Park

Lost Dutchman State Park is named after the legendary gold mine mysteriously lost after being discovered. It is located in the Sonoran Desert, at the bottom of the Superstition Mountains. The park has several trails connecting it with the mountain's wilderness and nearby national forest. You can do countless activities here - for instance, hike the Siphon Draw Trail or go on a nature walk along the Native Plant Trail. The weather mainly depends on the year's rainfall. Consequently, you might be welcomed with a dry desert-like atmosphere or a beautiful carpet of desert wildflowers. At Lost Dutchman State Park, you can experience a fun weekend of camping, exploring nature, and sightseeing birds and other wildlife animals.

The programs and events are also planned around the weather. In addition to the first-day hike, the organizers at this state park hold a full moon hike. So, this hike is for you if you're a night owl or love enjoying nature at night. Cultural heritage is promoted through various musical events where songwriters and musicians narrate the local stories. There's a "nature's bounty" program for people interested in botany and herbs every year. You will learn how the natives used various herbs and plants to treat ailments. This program is a history lesson and helps you shift your medicinal perspectives.

Another cool activity is the "firewise landscaping" program held at Lost Dutchman State Park. Master gardeners and landscapers teach you how to implement cool landscaping techniques in your gardens. A ton of other hiking opportunities are within the park's landscape for beginners and experienced hikers. Most hiking trails are easily accessible from the campgrounds and lead into the Superstition Mountains. Whether you visit the park during winter, spring, or fall, this state park is one of the best spots for hiking in all of Arizona.

In addition to hiking and nature trails, you can opt for wildlife excursions and bird watching to make your trip more interesting. Countless wildlife viewing opportunities are available all year in Lost Dutchman State Park. You can catch sight of coyotes, bobcats, jackrabbits, and deer. Most desert animals in this state are nocturnal, so the best time for these wildlife excursions is between late evenings and early mornings. On the other hand, bird watching has become increasingly popular in this state park, with almost all visitors partaking in this leisure activity. This activity is especially famous after winter, once the birds have migrated from the northern states.

The campground offers about 135 sites, developed and undeveloped. Around 68 sites have water and electric hook-ups and get reserved the earliest. Each site has a spacious picnic table, a fire ring, and a grill station. Camping and park rules that must be followed include:

- Camping permits must be displayed on your vehicles when entering the park. Always drive on the designated pathways.

- Quiet hours must be observed between 9 PM to 8 AM. Avoid making loud noises during this time.

- Moving, removing, or damaging artifacts or historical objects is strictly prohibited.

- Your pets must be leashed and not left unattended. Pets are not allowed in the park restrooms.

- No wood gathering is allowed within the park and nearby mountains. Fires are limited to the fire ring or grill station only.

- The maximum limit for your stay should not exceed 14 days.

- You must only camp in the designated areas, with a maximum of 10 people per campsite.

- To avoid getting your site forfeited when you're not around, leave something at your site to indicate your presence.

- Do not wash or repair your RV or any vehicle in the park or campground.

- Fireworks and firearms of any kind are strictly prohibited.

Considering that Arizona State is so interconnected, traveling through Arizona state parks is no less than an adventure that can be completed within a limited time. The diverse cultures, rich histories, and beautiful climates of Arizona state parks make them more exhilarating. Whether you're a dry-land-preferring individual or a water lover, Arizona state parks have all the variety. RV camping at these stunning state parks is an experience you don't want to miss. When camping out, you must follow the detailed guidelines each state park authority provides to ensure your trip goes smoothly.

# Chapter 4

# Wyoming State Parks

Wyoming is a vast expanse of nature untamed by modern society, boasting some of the most beautiful views in the entire country. This great land offers visitors a range of opportunities to explore its many wonders. One of the most popular ways to experience all Wyoming offers is by exploring its state parks. From fishing and camping to hiking, biking, and rock climbing, these parks provide an amazing array of activities for the whole family to enjoy. With dozens of state parks scattered throughout Cowboy State, there's sure to be something for everyone.

This chapter delves into what each state park offers and is intended as a comprehensive guide to planning your Wyoming state park adventures. This guide covers everything from parks, attractions, trails, and RV camping guidelines.

## State Parks

Wyoming offers a diverse range of state parks, from badlands and beaches to mountain peaks and alpine lakes. Among these parks are Yellowstone National Park, Glendo State Park, Grand Teton National Park, Fossil Butte National Monument, and Devils Tower National Monument. These parks are open year-round and offer various activities to appease outdoor enthusiasts.

Yellowstone National Park is perfect for people wanting to get up close and personal with nature. Grand Teton National Park offers spectacular views and plenty of activities like fishing, hiking, climbing, and camping. Devils Tower National Monument is great for stargazers or those looking to get an up-close look at the most iconic rock formation in the country. Fossil Butte National Monument is a great spot for people interested in learning about Wyoming's rich prehistoric history.

Wyoming state parks provide an array of attractions - from wildlife watching to white water rafting. Many parks feature natural wonders like geological formations, hot springs, and breathtaking views. Others offer more leisurely activities, such as biking trails, fishing spots, campsites, and picnicking areas. For example, Curt Gowdy State Park is the perfect spot for a day of fishing and canoeing.

Glendo State Park offers plenty of camping, biking, and horseback riding.

Wyoming is home to two national parks, Grand Teton and Yellowstone, which offer a wealth of outdoor recreation opportunities. From iconic landmarks like Old Faithful and the Grand Canyon of Yellowstone to many hiking trails, these parks are some of the most visited in all of Wyoming.

Wyoming has over 13 state parks, each offering a unique experience for visitors to enjoy. These parks come in all shapes and sizes and offer everything from fishing, camping, and hiking to skiing, snowmobiling, and more.

Whether you want a more extreme outdoor adventure or something more tranquil - Wyoming has it all.

## The Grand Teton National Park

It is one of the most popular state parks in Wyoming for a good reason. This stunning park boasts majestic peaks that rise over 13,000 feet above sea level and are visible everywhere in the state. As one of the most iconic landscapes in America, Grand Teton National Park attracts visitors worldwide.

Grand Teton is a paradise for outdoor enthusiasts and nature lovers, offering something for everyone to enjoy. Visitors can explore the park's many hiking trails that meander through forested landscapes and tranquil alpine meadows or journey down one of its numerous rivers in search of the perfect trout fishing spot.

Those looking for a more extreme adventure can try ice climbing, mountaineering, and backcountry skiing. During the winter months, snowmobiling is a popular activity in the park.

Grand Teton National Park has some truly spectacular sights for visitors. This park has everything from breathtaking mountain views and awe-inspiring sunsets to crystal blue lakes and abundant wildlife.

For those interested in photography, the iconic peaks of the Teton Range provide a spectacular backdrop to capture stunning scenic shots. Wildlife sightings are common throughout the park – keep your eyes open for bison, elk, moose, bears, and bald eagles.

With over 200 miles of trails, Grand Teton has many opportunities for visitors to explore the park. There is something for everyone, from short day hikes to multi-day backcountry trekking. Many trails offer spectacular views of the mountains and nearby lakes, making them perfect spots to enjoy the park's natural beauty.

### *RV Camping Guidelines*

RV camping in Wyoming state parks is a great way to explore the incredible natural beauty and adventure of this stunning setting.

- RV campers can enjoy all the amenities of their campsite, such as fire pits, picnic tables, and flush toilets.

- RVs up to 30 feet are allowed at all state parks. Some locations offer electrical hook-ups, allowing RV campers to stay comfortable and connected during their adventure.

- The camping sites are available on a first-come, first-served basis, so campers must plan ahead and arrive early to secure a spot.

- Some state parks offer visitors access to general stores, laundromats, gift shops, and showers, making the camping experience more enjoyable.

- When RV camping in a Wyoming state park, campers must always respect the environment and practice Leave No Trace principles to ensure their safety and preserve the beauty of these amazing natural sites.

## Glendo State Park

Glendo State Park is worth checking out if you want to explore the best of what Wyoming offers. Located on the banks of Glendo Reservoir and surrounded by stunning views of rolling hills and prairies, this state park offers a plethora of outdoor adventures for all ages.

It is one of the most popular Wyoming state parks. It's a great spot for RV camping, featuring amenities like electric and non-electric sites, flush toilets, and drinking water. With 50 miles of shoreline on the Glendo Reservoir, you'll have plenty to explore. The park boasts great trails, from easy walks along the reservoir to more challenging hikes up nearby bluffs. You can take in spectacular views of the lake and surrounding landscape and spot some local wildlife.

At Glendo State Park, you can explore the lake by boat or fish from the shore. There are many wildlife viewing opportunities, from bald eagles to deer and antelope. Species to spot in Glendo range from the Great Horned Owl to White-Tailed Deer and Bald Eagles; there's no shortage of animals to discover. You might come across Garter Snakes or Red-Tailed Hawks during your stay. The reservoir's waters are also home to some of Wyoming's most beautiful fish species, like Walleye and Northern Pike. For those looking for a more adventurous experience, the park offers rock climbing and rappelling on the reservoir's wall. You can enjoy a meal or relax in the shade of the park's many picnic areas and campgrounds.

If fishing is your passion, Glendo State Park is worth a visit. The lake is great for catching walleye, catfish, and smallmouth bass. For the more adventurous angler, you can find big game fish in the rugged areas nearby. At Glendo State Park, the possibilities for fun and recreation are endless.

Archery, swimming, boating, wildlife viewing, and camping are other activities to enjoy at this beautiful Wyoming park. There's something here for everyone - so make sure to check it out on your next road trip around the USA!

## RV Camping Guidelines

Weather permitting, Glendo State Park is open year-round. For RV camping, check the park's website for availability and guidelines. Be aware of the following rules and regulations before setting up camp:

- RV sites are limited to a maximum of 40-foot, including trailer and tow vehicles

- All vehicles must have valid registration and license plates

- No fires are allowed in fire rings, or grates other than designated areas

- Dump stations are located near the campground entrance

- All camping equipment and belongings must be removed from the campsite upon departure.

So, if you're planning a road trip to Wyoming, check out Glendo State Park - it's a great spot for camping, fishing, and exploring the great outdoors. With its stunning views, excellent amenities, and plenty to do and see, it will be one of the highlights of your trip.

## Edness K. Wilkins State Park

Look no further than Edness K. Wilkins state park in Wyoming for a unique state park experience. This park is a nature lover's dream, with many natural attractions to explore and enjoy.

The state park is located near Casper in north-central Wyoming, making driving easy. Situated on the North Platte River, it's surrounded by lush vegetation and stunning views of the river and nearby hills. It was named after Edness Kimball Wilkins, the first women speaker in Wyoming's legislature.

At Edness K. Wilkins state park, visitors can expect many outdoor activities, from nature watching to hiking and biking through the park's peaceful woodlands. The park's most popular attraction is its hike to the top of Laramie Peak, which offers stunning views of the surrounding landscape. The park is home to diverse wildlife, including beaver, mule deer, and bald eagles. The river offers kayaking and canoeing opportunities if you're feeling adventurous.

Many RV camping options are available if you plan to visit the park. The campground features full hook-up sites, tent camping, cabins, picnic tables, fire pits, and restrooms. Visitors must follow specific guidelines when visiting the park.

### *RV Camping Guidelines*

- Park in designated camping areas only

- Campfires must be in a designated fire pit

- All campers must take out their trash

- Quiet hours must be obeyed

- Alcoholic beverages are prohibited

- No swimming is allowed in the river

Edness K. Wilkins state park has something for everyone, offering a perfect combination of outdoor activities and stunning scenery. Adventurers, nature lovers, and campers will find something they enjoy here. So, explore Edness K. Wilkins state park for a fun and unique Wyoming experience.

## Yellowstone National Park

It is the largest national park in the United States, expanding over three states. Boasting some of the most unique natural features in the world, Yellowstone is one of Wyoming's premier destinations for outdoor recreation.

The iconic Old Faithful geyser erupts regularly throughout the year, attracting visitors worldwide to witness this spectacular event. Other natural wonders, like the Mammoth hot spring, provide visitors with several opportunities to explore this beautiful landscape.

The park is home to abundant wildlife and stunning thermal features. Hayden Valley and Lamar Valley are popular spots for spotting bison, elk, wolves, bears, and the occasional grizzly bear.

Yellowstone has many activities for visitors to enjoy. Fishing in Yellowstone National Park is a popular recreational activity for visitors. Angling has been an important part of the park's history, and regulations are in place to ensure fish resources are properly managed and preserved. All anglers over 16 must purchase a permit to fish, with options ranging from three-day ($15) to seasonal ($35). Younger anglers are permitted to fish but under adult supervision.

Fishing regulations restrict using bait, specify season opening and closing dates, and the size and number limits for each species. Certain areas are closed for visitors to protect endangered species and provide scenic viewing. Yellowstone's beautiful landscape and abundant wild fish make fishing a wonderful way to enjoy the park.

You can also enjoy biking on designated routes. These routes are designated gravel roads open to bicycle rides and automotive vehicles. Many trails are restricted to foot and bicycle traffic only so visitors can enjoy the surrounding nature. Some unpaved paths are specifically reserved for bicycles.

### *RV Camping Guidelines*

RV camping in Yellowstone national park is allowed, but a few guidelines must be followed.

- RVs must keep to designated roads and sites; no off-roading is permitted.

- Camping is limited to 14 days during 30 days; vehicles exceeding 25 feet in length or 8 feet in width are not permitted.

- Fires are only allowed in designated fire pits.

- All human waste must be disposed of properly and hygienically.

- Bicycles are permitted on specific trails only.

- Visitors must adhere to the park's wildlife viewing and activity regulations - for instance, not throwing anything into thermal features or willfully approaching or disturbing wildlife.

## Buffalo Bill State Park

This is a stunning park in northwestern Wyoming where you can enjoy RV camping. With views of the Absaroka Range and Yellowstone National Park, this state park is a popular destination for visitors to explore Wyoming's most beautiful wilderness. Buffalo Bill Reservoir features a 350-foot dam; it was once the world's tallest dam.

At Buffalo Bill State Park, visitors can immerse themselves in nature's beauty while partaking in various outdoor activities such as biking, hiking, and camping. The park offers several trails for hikers, ranging from short, easy trails to long, difficult ones. Buffalo Bill State Park provides plenty of options for camping at the two campsites, North Fork, and North Shore, with limited reservable sites.

The park provides beautiful views of the surrounding area and a variety of wildlife, including deer, bighorn sheep, and antelope, for visitors to enjoy.

Besides admiring the scenic shoreline and taking a boat ride around its tranquil waters, visitors can also explore Shoshone Canyon and learn more at the park's visitor center, which features historical exhibits. Whether you want a day of leisure or adventure, Buffalo Bill State Park offers something for everyone.

### *RV Camping Guidelines*

RV campers are welcome at Buffalo Bill State Recreation Area and must abide by the rules and regulations of the park.

- Guests can choose from electric, electric plus, and basic camping pads with 50-amp hook-ups available.

- During winter, some facilities and amenities are closed.

- All campers must check in at the visitor center before setting up their campsite.

- All RVs must be registered, and visitors must purchase a valid camping pass before their stay. Visitors are expected to keep their vehicle and campsite clean during their stay and leave the area as they found it upon departure.

- All pets must be kept on a leash at all times and must be cleaned up after.

- Fires are permitted in designated fire pits. All fires must be extinguished before leaving the site.

## Bear River State Park

Bear River State Park is a stunning natural area on the edge of Evanston, close to the Utah border. Locals and tourists can enjoy this tranquil oasis encompassing both sides of the river. Visitors can explore its lush landscapes, with picturesque overlooks, trails perfect for exploring, and peaceful picnic spots dotted throughout.

The park is a great place to absorb nature. It is home to various wildlife, including bison and elk, that can be spotted wandering the grounds. Other animals like deer, moose, and bears have been seen in the park. Since its clean-up in the 90s, Bear River has become a popular destination for activities such as picnicking, bird watching, hiking, biking, skiing, and rollerblading.

The park has a visitor's center providing educational information on the area and over 300 acres of land perfect for exploring. Three miles of foot trails include paved and unpaved paths, with an arched bridge crossing over the river. During winter, many trails are suitable for cross-country skiing and snowshoeing. Unfortunately, Bear River does not allow overnight camping, making it a great day-trip destination.

No matter what time of year you visit, Bear River State Park offers a truly unique experience for all who visit. With its stunning landscapes, abundant wildlife, and welcoming atmosphere, this natural area is perfect for escaping the hustle and bustle of daily life.

Bear River State Park is an idyllic location for nature lovers and outdoor enthusiasts. With its abundance of wildlife, trails perfect for exploration, and visitor's center offering educational information. There's something at Bear River State Park to delight every visitor.

## Hot Springs State Park

Hot Springs State Park is another must-see destination in Wyoming. This state park is a natural hot spring near Thermopolis and the Big Horn Mountains, famous for its mineral hot springs, abundant wildlife, and famous terraces.

Terraces are Hot Springs State park's most iconic feature. This natural formation begins near the mineral hot springs and cascades down, creating a picturesque display. The terraces are made from travertine, a limestone deposited by the hot springs. Depending on the minerals, they range from pink to turquoise.

The hot springs are another major highlight of this park. It features mineral-rich thermal waters believed to have healing properties and is a unique experience for visitors.

Wildlife is abundant in the park, including elk, deer, big horn sheep, and turkeys that roam freely. Nature trails for a more intimate experience with the wildlife are available.

The park has several attractions, including the ¼ mile-long boardwalk, winding its way around an oasis of hot springs and mineral-rich ponds. Visitors can enjoy several sightseeing opportunities, such as geysers, bubbling hot pools, and wildlife. Additionally, the park features interpretive programs explaining the natural history and geology behind these thermal wonders.

Hot Springs State Park offers a range of facilities for visitors to enjoy. It has 6.2 miles of trails, ideal for hiking or walking, with some areas suitable for those with limited mobility.

The park has picnic areas and a visitors' center. Visitors can enjoy observing bison up close during their morning feeding time. No camping is allowed at the park since it is designated as a day-use area, but it offers plenty for a day of fun and relaxation.

Hot Springs State Park offers a unique geological experience pleasing to locals and visitors. Its easy accessibility makes it a great destination for everyone; whether it's wildlife, geothermal features, or a peaceful spot to relax, this park has something for everyone.

Wyoming is beautiful. Its parks are full of wonderful landscapes, wildlife, and activities. From Buffalo Bill State Park's serene waters to Bear River State Park's lush pathways, there is something for everyone to explore the outdoors. Whether seeking a relaxing day in nature or an invigorating adventure, Wyoming has the perfect state park. So, pack your gear and head out to explore these beloved parks.

# Chapter 5

# Washington State Parks

Glacial peaks, rivers, and lush green rainforests can all be found in Washington. Washington State is a sanctuary for outdoor enthusiasts and adventurers because of its diverse natural environment. The Washington State Parks and Recreation Commission oversees more than 140 parks. You won't need to seek further because we cover the best state parks in Washington, their significant attractions, and rules for RV camping in this chapter.

## Olympic National Park

The Olympic National Park in northwest Washington covers almost a million acres and is home to various ecosystems, including old-growth forests, rocky coastlines, and snow-capped mountain peaks. Although most park sections are open all year, inclement weather could make it impossible to reach mountain peaks.

**Hiking:** The park offers numerous hiking trails for hikers of various experience levels and interests, from moderate nature hikes to strenuous backcountry treks. The Sol Duc Falls Trail, the Hoh Rain Forest Trail, and Hurricane Ridge Trail are a few of the popular trails.

**Backpacking:** A variety of backpacking routes are available, from simple overnight excursions to more difficult multi-day journeys. The park's varied terrain, which features old-growth woods, snow-capped mountain peaks, and a rocky coastline, is enjoyed by backpackers and adventurers.

**Rock Climbing:** Several rock climbing routes range from manageable to challenging technical climbs. The Lower Town Wall and the Upper Town Wall are popular climbing locations that should be on your to-do list if you are a rock climber.

**Beachcombing:** Another fun activity is exploring the park's rocky shoreline in search of shells, agates, and other natural treasures.

**Bird Watching:** A plethora of bird species, including bald eagles, ospreys, and puffins, can be seen in the park. Charming locations to see birds include the Sol Duc Valley and the Hoh Rain Forest.

### *Olympic National Park's Trails*

**Hurricane Ridge Trail**: This mesmerizing trail ascends Hurricane Ridge to its peak, where you can take in sweeping vistas of the Olympic Mountains and the Strait of Juan de Fuca. The track is around 2.6 miles round trip and has moderate difficulty.

**Hoh Rain Forest Route**: This short trail winds through the stunning Hoh Rain Forest, a park-located temperate rainforest. The trail is 1.2 miles long and filled with breathtaking landscapes and pleasant terrain.

**The trail to Sol Duc Falls:** This easy trail takes hikers to the park's stunning Sol Duc Falls and stretches 3 miles.

## RV Camping Guidelines

- Only the park manages Fairholme, Mora, Hoh Rain forest, and Kalaloch campgrounds and accepts reservations through a state-run official channel.

- The Washington State Park and Recreation Commission's website offers various campsite services. The park's other campgrounds are all first-come, first-served.

- Contact the National Park officials to reserve a group camping site.

- Wild animals might enter in quest of food and other scented goods if not securely guarded. So, ensure to wash your dishes, dispose of trash, and maintain a spotless campground. All food should be kept in an animal-proof storage locker or a car's trunk.

- Visitors can gather dead and downed wood with a maximum diameter of six inches for firewood. The campground's neighborhood has places where you can gather firewood.

- The log cabin resort and RV campground have showers and laundry facilities, whereas park-operated sites do not.

- The Long Island Resort and the Sol Duc Hot Springs are the only campsites offering electricity and electrical hook-ups, other campsites in the park don't.

- The available RV space in campsites varies from 21 to 35 feet. Contact the visitor centers at the campsite parks for more information.

- Olympic National Park policies

- Campgrounds accept pets, but they must be kept on a leash while there. The Peabody Creek, Madison Falls, Kalaloch, and Spruce Railroad Trails do not allow pets.

- For the animal's health and your personal safety, refrain from feeding wild animals.

- When visiting the park, avoid disturbing the wildlife.

- You can only camp for a week to two weeks in the busiest months.

- A maximum of 8 persons per location is permitted.

## Mount Rainier National Park

This park is in the heart of Washington, home to the magnificent Mount Rainier, the state's tallest mountain and an active volcano. Alpine meadows, glaciers, and old-growth woods make up the park's scenery, a haven for outdoor enthusiasts.

**Hiking:** The park is home to a diverse network of hiking paths, ranging from leisurely strolls in the woods to challenging journeys through the wilderness, suitable for hikers of all skill levels. The most popular trails include The Skyline Trail, Nisqually Vista Trail, and Wonderland Trail.

**Rock Climbing:** The Gibraltar Rock and the Elysian Fields are two well-known climbing locations where climbers from all over the country enjoy these challenging locations.

**Climbing:** The park offers many mountaineering routes and is home to Mount Rainier, an active volcano. The park's alpine meadows, glaciers, and snow-capped peaks attract mountaineers. The Paradise Loop Road, which provides sweeping views of the mountain and the surrounding area, is one of the park's picturesque routes.

**Viewing Wildlife:** Various animals, including elk, mountain goats, and marmots, can be found throughout the park.

### Mount Rannier National Park Trails

**Skyline Trail:** This path ascends Mount Rainier, offering sweeping vistas of the region as it descends. The 9.5-mile trail is challenging and complex.

**The Nisqually Vista Trail:** It is a short hike that ends at a vista point with views of the Nisqually Glacier and the surrounding area. The trail is roughly one mile long and provides a magnificent landscape view.

**Wonderland Trek**: This challenging trail encircles Mount Rainier and offers a variety of scenery and mountain views. The track is 93 miles long.

### RV Camping Guidelines

- Each of the four campgrounds offers different levels of amenities. First come, first served applies to all campgrounds. However, reservations can be made for the Cougar Rock and Ohanapecosh Rock campgrounds via the Washington Recreation Commission website.

- Only specified campsites offer camping; sleeping outside a vehicle or in a campground is not permitted.

- Six campers and two tents are the maximum allowed.

- There are defined places for RVs, not elsewhere.

- The campgrounds provide group tenting spaces.

- There is a two-week camping maximum at built campgrounds and a 28-day camping maximum elsewhere in the park. At noon, guests must vacate the park.

- Shops where you can buy firewood are on-site. Burning harvested wood or purchasing wood from somewhere else can be unhealthy and is not permitted in the park.

- The campgrounds allow leashed or in-caged pets.

- Motorbikes and bicycles are permitted at the location.

## North Cascades National Park

Northwest Washington's North Cascades National Park is renowned for its rough, mountainous terrain and impressive glaciers. The park is a stunning and distinctive location because of its diverse landscape, including forests, alpine meadows, and glacial lakes.

**Hiking:** The Cascade Pass Trail, the Easy Pass Trail, and the Maple Pass Loop Trail are well-liked trails.

**Rock Climbing:** The park offers many rock climbing routes, from manageable levels to challenging technical climbs. Eldorado Peak and the South Early Winter are popular locations for climbing.

**Backpacking:** The park offers several backpacking routes, from simple overnight excursions to more difficult multi-day journeys. The park's untamed, mountainous terrain, highlighted by glaciers, alpine meadows, and old-growth forests, is perfect for hikers and backpackers who love to wander in nature.

**Fishing:** Several fish species, including rainbow trout, cutthroat trout, and Dolly Varden, are abundant in the park's waters. Fishing is excellent in glacial lakes and streams.

**Viewing Wildlife:** A variety of animals, such as bears, mountain goats, and marmots, can be found in the park. The forests and alpine meadows are excellent places to see wildlife.

### Trails to Explore

**Maple Pass Loop Trail:** This easy trail passes through alpine meadows while providing views of the surrounding peaks. The course is roughly 7.2 miles long.

**Easy Pass Trail:** This trail passes through forests, providing a serene landscape view, and is roughly 6.4 miles long. The trail includes scenic views from Granite creek, opening into a basin. The trail ends at the easy pass.

**Cascade Pass Trail:** This moderate trail is about 6.2 miles round trip and takes you through unchartered land protected to preserve its beauty and thriving wildlife.

## *RV Camping Guidelines*

- Depending on the season and weather conditions, several campgrounds in the park might be accessible. Therefore, always contact the park authority and make a reservation if you intend to visit.

- Overnight camping is allowed only in select campsites. Parking or camping in areas other than the park complex is prohibited.

- The occupancy is limited to 8 people, three tents, and two vehicles.

- Firewood, gas, and electrical services are unavailable at the park and can be accessed by visiting the nearest town of Marbel Mount.

- Two weeks of camping are allowed from July to September. A 30-day stay is allowed throughout the rest of the year.

## Deception Pass State Park

Located on Whidbey Island in northwest Washington, this state park is known for its stunning coastline, forests, and beaches. The park's beautiful beaches and forests make it a great place to relax and enjoy nature.

**Hiking:** The park has a variety of hiking trails to suit different skill levels and interests, ranging from easy nature walks to more challenging routes. Some popular tracks include the Lighthouse Point Trail and the Cranberry Lake Trail.

**Fishing:** The park is home to various fish species, including salmon, steelhead, and trout. The park's lakes and streams are great places to fish.

**Beachcombing:** The park's beautiful coastline is a great place to explore and look for treasures like shells, agates, and other natural treasures.

**Boating:** The park has several boat launches, and visitors can enjoy various boating activities, including kayaking, canoeing, and stand-up paddleboarding. Due to changing weather conditions, it might not be possible to do boating activities. Therefore, contact the park authorities before visiting the park.

**Picnicking:** The park has several picnic areas, and visitors can enjoy a leisurely meal surrounded by the park's beautiful forests and beaches. In-park stores are available if you are running short on picnic supplies.

### *Trails in Deception Pass State Park*

**Lighthouse Point Trail:** This easy trail leads to a viewpoint overlooking Deception Pass and the surrounding coastline. The course is about 0.5 miles round trip.

**Cranberry Lake Trail**: This moderate trail leads through forests and along the shores of Cranberry Lake. About 2.5 kilometers round trip make up the trail. Several hiking challenges are created by the hiking community visiting the park to engage fellow hikers. The CL50 challenge is a famous and challenging task for anyone.

### *RV Camping Guidelines*

- There are more than 150 tent sites, hundreds of parietal hook-up sites, and five biker and hiking sites.

- A group campsite accommodating a maximum of 50 people is available, charging you a flat fee for a grassy camping site, flush toilets, a firewood place, and picnic shelters.

- The park is open all year for camping. However, camping at only the quarry pond campground in winter is allowed.

## Fort Worden State Park

Fort Worden State Park is in northwest Washington, home to historic military fortifications, gorgeous beaches, and forests. It is situated on the Olympic Peninsula. The park has a distinctly rich history and stunning surroundings, making it a must-visit place for camping and exploration.

**Hiking:** The park offers a range of hiking trails to accommodate different skill levels and interests. The Madrona Way Trail and the Point Wilson Lighthouse Trail stand out from the rest of the trails due to their stunning landscape.

**Fishing:** Salmon, steelhead, and trout are among the many fish species in the park if you want to enjoy fishing.

**Beachcombing:** The park's stunning coastline is a beautiful location to explore and hunt for artifacts like agates, shells, and other natural treasures.

**Boating**: Kayaking, canoeing, and stand-up paddleboarding are a few boating activities available to visitors at the park's numerous boat launches.

### *Fort Worden State Park's trails*

**The Artillery Hill Trail**: A short path winds through Fort Worden's old defenses and provides views of the neighborhood. The trail is around 1 mile long.

**Point Wilson Lighthouse Walk:** This easy trail leads to the Point Wilson Lighthouse with coastline views. The track is roughly 1.5 miles long.

### *RV Camping Guidelines*

- Three RV parks, namely the Pioneer trails, North Whidbey, and Cliffside RV parks, have amenities like water, sewer, and electrical hookups.

- The RV parks provide WiFi and are pet-friendly.

## Mount St. Helens National Volcanic Monument

Situated in southwest Washington, this park is home to Mount St. Helens, an active volcano that last erupted in 1980. You can hike to the monument, exploring the remnants of a volcanic eruption after almost 43 years.

**Rock Climbing:** The South Sisters and the Climber's Bivouac are popular climbing locations. They require a climber's permit if a hiker wants to climb above 4800 feet. Climbing permits are self-issued on-site from the 1st of December to the 30th of March. Whereas 30 permits are issued from the 1st of April to the 30th of November.

**Mountain biking:** The park offers plenty of mountain biking tracks, from straightforward loops to more complicated circuits. The Ape Canyon Trail and the Smith Creek Trails provide mountain biking rides on specific weekdays. The schedule can be obtained from the park management.

### *Trails in Mount St. Helens*

**Hummocks Walk:** The trail travels through the hummocks, debris mounds left from Mount St. Helens' 1980 eruption. Throughout the 2-mile roundtrip walk are views of the surrounding area.

**The challenging Harry's Ridge Trail**: The ridge trail provides panoramic views of Mount St. Helens and the surrounding area as it ascends to the ridge. The trail is roughly 5.5 kilometers and provides stunning views of the wildflowers and greenery.

**The Monitor Ridge Trail:** It's a challenging path that ascends Mount St. Helens and provides a magnificent view of the surrounding rocky landscape. The trail's total distance is roughly 8.8 miles.

**Lewis and Clark Trail State Park:** This state park is situated in eastern Washington and traces the path the Lewis and Clark expedition took when they explored the region in the early 1800s.

**The Snake River Walk:** It's a short, simple trail with views of the Snake River. The course is four miles.

**Chief Timothy Park Trail:** This short path travels through the park's Chief Timothy Park, a historic location. The route covers a distance of three miles.

## *RV Camping Guidelines*

- The Gifford Pinchot National Forest includes the Mount St. Helens National Volcanic Monument. The area is divided into South, West, and East Sides, each having unique trails, viewpoints, and several RV campgrounds and hundreds of campsites.

- Most RV camping is carried out on the Southside and overlooks PacifiCorp.

- Regardless of the campground, it's best to make a reservation a few months before visiting the park.

- The Swift Forest Camp, Iron creek, Eagle Cliff, and Beaver Bay are popular campgrounds with dozens of campsites, distinct landscapes, and viewpoints to enjoy.

- Most campgrounds stay open throughout the year, but some only provide camping facilities for a few months. For example, the Swift Forest Camp is only available in October and November.

- Some campgrounds provide amenities like toilets, showers, WiFi, and electric and water hookups. For others, you must pack the necessary gear for a real adventure.

## Riverside State Park

Eastern Washington's Riverside State Park is well-known for its stunning forests, meadows, and rivers. Boating, fishing, picnics, biking, and horseback riding are some activities you can enjoy while visiting the park.

### Trails in Riverside State Park

**Trails in Bowl and Pitcher Walk:** This easy trail takes you to the park's unusual rock feature known as the Bowl and Pitcher. The trail is roughly 6 miles long.

**Route in Nine Mile Recreation Area:** This short trail passes the Nine Mile Recreation Area and provides views of the surroundings. The trail is two miles.

**Sun Lakes-Dry Falls trails:** The Sun Lakes Trail travels through Sun Lakes, a picturesque region with lakes and woodlands for two miles. The route to Dry Falls, a sizable waterfall no longer with flowing water, is short and straightforward. The trail is roughly one mile long.

## *RV Camping Guidelines*

- Plenty of RV campgrounds are available, some providing amenities, others allowing you to tap into nature in its true form.

- The roads inside the park are well-maintained. However, people with large vehicles should be cautious, especially in winter.

- Bowl and Pitcher, Lake Spokane, and Nine Mile Recreation campgrounds are famous sites for RV camping.

- It's best to contact the park authorities and reserve your spot in advance.

## Palouse Falls State Park

Palouse Falls is a stunning waterfall in Palouse Falls State Park, giving the park its unique name. Various activities are available in the park, including hiking, camping, fishing, bird watching, and geology excursions.

## *Palouse Falls State Park's trails*

**Palouse Falls Walk:** This short trail goes to the park's stunning waterfall, Palouse Fall, and is roughly 0.5 miles long. It's considered a challenging trail, and you'll encounter many visitors since it's a popular hiking trail. The best time to visit is between February and the end of October.

**Palouse Falls Overlook Trail:** A length of 0.25 miles, this easy trail takes you through mesmerizing views of Palouse Falls and the surrounding areas.

### *RV Camping Guidelines*

- You can get entry via a day pass or an annual discover pass of varying fees.

- The pass should always be displayed on the vehicle's windshield. Failure to display the pass can lead to a $99 fine.

- The parking length is 20 feet maximum.

- Available are 11 tent-only campsites and one site for disabled people.

- Several sheltered and unsheltered picnic tables are available.

- Restrooms are available near all camping areas.

- Contact the park authorities for more information on available campsites.

The information in this chapter briefly overviews activities in these state parks. Most parks are spread over acres of land and have several RV camping sites, hiking trails, and other activities like boating, wildlife viewing, birdwatching, beachcombing, and much more. The activities might be available elsewhere, depending primarily on the weather conditions. Therefore, contact the park authorities before visiting a state park. While some trails are free, others require a small fee charged by the park authorities.

Furthermore, most Washington state parks have similar RV guidelines and regulations. The difference is the available amenities, services provided by the park, and the fee. The state government runs some campgrounds; others are private-run campgrounds, providing facilities like water, electrical, and sewer hookups. This chapter aids you in exploring Washington state parks and camping out with peace of mind.

# Chapter 6

# California State Parks

It can be confusing figuring out which California State Park is best for RV camping. There are many incredible parks to choose from, making narrowing down your options difficult. Fortunately, this chapter provides rig campers with detailed information on the top parks in the state, giving potential campers a thorough understanding of their options for finding a spot for a vacation or spontaneous getaway. From beaches and deserts to coastal wildlands, this guide offers descriptions and reviews to help you pick the right park based on scenery and other important factors like distance to nearby restaurants and activities. So, don't let confusion get in the way; this chapter will confidently lead you toward the perfect outdoor camping adventure.

## Emerald Bay State Park

Emerald Bay State Park is located in the southwestern corner of Lake Tahoe, California. It's a picturesque notch of the lake with breathtaking views of the surrounding Sierra Nevada Mountains and deep blue waters. The park features beaches, Tahoe's only island, Fannette Island, and an unexpected Scandinavian-style stone castle.

The Eagle Point Campground offers tent camping, RV spots, and amenities like bathrooms, showers, picnic tables, and fire rings. Electric hook-ups are available for RVs at some sites. The campground provides direct access to the Rubicon Trail—a popular hiking trail through Emerald Bay and the adjacent Desolation Wilderness area. Other popular activities include kayaking on Fannette Island, scuba diving, and fishing.

*RV Camping Guidelines*

Some important rules and guidelines must be followed when camping in the Emerald Bay State Park.

- RVs must have a minimum of 25 feet between them and other vehicles or campsites.

- All campers must register with the ranger station before setting up.

- All campfires must be contained within fire rings provided by park officials.

- Pets are allowed on leashes in designated areas only.

With its beautiful beaches, lush forests, and breathtaking views, Emerald Bay State Park is an ideal destination for outdoor recreation enthusiasts near Lake Tahoe. From hiking trails and kayaking trips to scuba diving excursions and comfortable RV camping spots—there's something for everyone to enjoy. Remember to follow the park's guidelines and regulations when visiting.

## Julia Pfeiffer Burns State Park

Located on California's Big Sur coast, Julia Pfeiffer Burns State Park is a stunning park known for its secluded beach cove and breathtaking scenery. This park offers spectacular views of the Pacific Ocean, with rugged cliffs stretching along the shoreline. The 80-acre McWay Creek falls into a sandy beach beautifully framed by the rocky landscape. While no visitors are allowed onto the beach due to its dangerous terrain, an adjoining trail provides a perfect view of the iconic waterfall.

Other attractions of this state park include miles of hiking trails, panoramic vistas of ocean sunsets and redwood forests, and plenty of wildlife viewing opportunities. Visitors can cross over creeks on bridges, observe the park's plentiful deer, and spot whales in the sparkling blue ocean.

Campers who stay in Julia Pfeiffer Burns State Park will enjoy the many amenities, including an RV campground with full hook-ups for up to 48 RVs. Guests can take advantage of the campground's showers, restrooms, picnic tables, and fire pits. Visitors are asked to follow all camping guidelines while enjoying their stay to keep this beautiful park safe.

Meanwhile, those looking to explore the area further will be pleased with the number of trails offered at Julia Pfeiffer Burns State Park. Top trails include Ewoldsen Trail—which includes a waterfall and creek, and the Tan Bark Trail, Treebones Trail, Old Coast Road Trail, and Partington Cove Trail. With so many trails to explore, there is something for everyone.

### *RV Camping Guidelines*

If you're visiting with your RV, read the park's guidelines to ensure your trip is as smooth and enjoyable as possible.

- The park requires vehicles no more than 25 feet in length.
- Vehicles must stay on existing roads and parking areas.
- Oversized vehicles like trailers carrying bikes or kayaks must be towed by an RV that meets the size requirements.

- There are no hook-ups for RVs, so bring plenty of water for you, your companions, and your RV.

- Camping fees must be paid within 30 minutes after occupancy, so have a game plan ready when you arrive.

Whether RV camping or exploring nearby trails, Julia Pfeiffer Burns State Park is a nature lover's paradise. Its spectacular views of Big Sur's rugged coastline make it an unforgettable destination for campers looking for a peaceful retreat.

## Humboldt Redwoods State Park

Humboldt Redwoods State Park is located in northern California and spans more than 53,000 acres of ancient redwood groves. It's the largest old-growth coastal redwood forest in the world, with some trees reaching up to 379 feet tall. The park is situated along the Avenue of the Giants, a 31-mile scenic highway that winds through towering forests.

The park offers tent camping, RV camping, and backcountry camping sites and cabins for rent. Campers can enjoy swimming pools and hot showers at various campgrounds throughout the park. Popular attractions in Humboldt Redwoods State Park include Founders Grove Nature Trail, home to the fallen Dyerville Giant; the 4-mile-long Bull Creek Flats trail, which follows the banks of Redwood Creek and the Rockefeller Forest, a 13,000-acre ancient redwood forest. Humboldt Redwoods State Park has several RV camping areas offering stunning views of towering redwoods.

## RV Camping Guidelines

- Vehicles over 20 feet in length or wider than 8 feet must stay on designated roads.

- Vehicles must park in marked sites.

- All RVs must have a valid California registration or proof of ownership while staying at the park.

- Fees vary depending on campsite selection and the number of people in each party staying overnight.

- Tent camping fees range from $35 to $45.

- RV camping fees range from $45 to $55.

Humboldt Redwoods State Park offers a wide variety of activities and attractions for campers. In addition to the many trails that meander through the park's forests, visitors can enjoy swimming and boating on nearby rivers and streams, fishing in designated areas, and exploring historical sites like the abandoned gold mines of Cuneo Creek. The park is home to nearly 200 bird species, making it an ideal spot for bird watching. Humboldt Redwoods State Park has something for everyone.

## McArthur-Burney Falls Memorial State Park

McArthur-Burney Falls Memorial State Park is located in the Shasta Cascade region of Northern California and lies at the base of the majestic Cascade Range. Home to a stunning 129-foot waterfall fed by underground springs and Burney Creek, this park offers visitors unparalleled views of nature's beauty. Visitors have access to five miles of hiking trails—including one segment of the Pacific Crest Trail—traversing the Cascade Range with multiple vistas for campers, hikers, and sightseers.

The campground features RV spots with full hook-ups (water, sewer, 30/50 amp electric) and tent sites with access to restrooms and showers. Reservations are first come, first served, or reserved up to six months in advance.

The park boasts multiple attractions and sights, including a clear blue spring-fed swimming hole, nature walks, numerous picnic areas, a boat launch onto Lake Britton—the largest man-made lake in California—and the Falls Creek Nature Trail. The Falls Creek Nature Trail is an easy 1.2-mile loop along the western edge of Burney Creek and features some of the most beautiful views of McArthur-Burney's namesake falls.

McArthur-Burney Falls Memorial State Park offers additional activities, such as fishing, kayaking, and canoeing on Lake Britton, bird and wildlife watching, stargazing from their campground sites at night, and several interpretive programs.

### *RV Camping Guidelines*

- If you plan to stay in the RV spots, you must follow a few guidelines.

- All campers must check in with the park Ranger at least one hour before sunset.

- All campfires must be contained within the fire rings provided by the Park. No pets are allowed on the trails, beaches, or watercraft (motorized and non-motorized).

- All posted speed limits on Lake Britton must be obeyed.

- The maximum RV length is 40 feet.

- Generators are only allowed from 8 am to 9 pm.

- Campers must remain vigilant in cleaning up residue after their stay, including dumping wastewater.

- Before entering the park, vehicles exceeding 10,000 pounds must follow special instructions on how to enter and what roads are accessible.

- Campers must review all the regulations before visiting the park for a safe and enjoyable experience without disruption.

McArthur-Burney Falls Memorial State Park is truly a treasured jewel nestled in Northern California's Cascade Range, offering visitors an unforgettable experience amid some of nature's most awe-inspiring wonders. McArthur-Burney Falls Memorial State Park is a must-see destination for outdoor enthusiasts, from breathtaking views of its namesake falls to multiple recreation opportunities.

## Crystal Cove State Park

Crystal Cove State Park is a coastal paradise of 3.2 miles of beach, tide pools, coves, and canyons in Newport Beach, California. The 1,400-acre park is perfect for camping, hiking, birdwatching, and horseback riding.

Crystal Cove offers RV campgrounds and tent campsites with stunning ocean views from the terraced bluffs above the beach. The RV campground features 20 spots with full hook-ups that accommodate RVs up to 35 feet long. A shower facility, picnic tables, and fire rings are available at all sites. The tent sites offer a peaceful atmosphere surrounded by trees and shrubs, ideal for the gardeners in your group or family.

Some of the major attractions and sights to explore while camping at Crystal Cove is The Beachcomber, a 1930s cottage with an oceanfront deck. El Moro Canyon Trail offers amazing views of the canyon and its surrounding vegetation. Pelican Point is home to a large variety of seabirds, and the tide pools, which provide a unique opportunity for close-up viewing of marine life.

The park features several trails that range from easy strolls along the beach to more challenging climbs through El Moro Canyon. Popular trails include Reef Point Trail, Tupelo Trail, and Rattlesnake Trail. For horseback riders, there is a dedicated equestrian day-use area.

### *RV Camping Guidelines*

When camping at Crystal Cove, please remember to respect the park and its wildlife by following these guidelines:

- Set up camp in a designated area.

- Do not cut down trees or damage natural resources.

- Some areas are closed for preservation purposes.

- Always be mindful of wildlife.

- Vehicles must have a current California Department of Parks and Recreation vehicle day-use permit and proof of reservation in possession as they enter the park.

- Like any vehicle, RV drivers must follow all park rules of the road when entering and exiting the campsite.

- Observe quiet hours from 10 pm-6 am. No amplified sound or offensive music is permitted after 10 pm, so keep it quiet while RVing.

Crystal Cove State Park is a paradise for outdoor enthusiasts who seek exploration and adventure with breathtaking ocean views. Whether you visit for a few days or plan an extended stay, it will be an unforgettable experience.

## Russian Gulch State Park

Russian Gulch State Park, California, is a beautiful park south of Mendocino. With its rugged and stunning coastline, this park offers unparalleled views of the Pacific Ocean from numerous overlooks dotting the Blufftop Headlands Trail. The Devil's Punchbowl is a must-see, an impressive collapsed sea cave with crashing waves and dramatic scenery.

For those seeking trails, Fern Canyon Trail is a great option for all hiking levels. It follows a rippling creek through a lush moss-shrouded redwood forest and leads to a 36-foot waterfall plunging into a forested grotto. Other trails in the park include Mailliard Redwoods Loop Trail, Russian Gulch Creek Trail, and Headlands Trail.

This park offers camping for tent and RV campers. You can find different campsites with fire pits, picnic tables, and access to vault toilets and drinking water. Various RV spots are available at the Russian Gulch Campground.

### *RV Camping Guidelines*

- No blackwater or greywater discharge allowed (all tanks must be emptied off-site).

- Generator use is restricted from 8 pm - 10 am.

- No dumping or washing anything on site.

- All pets must be leashed at all times.

- Stays are limited to a maximum of 15 days within a calendar year.

- Specific designated camping spots are available throughout the park on a first-come, first-serve basis.

- RV campers must not leave any trace behind by disposing of food scraps, refraining from leaving firewood behind, and not driving on vegetation or entering closed areas.

Remember to check all applicable regulations for Russian Gulch before you book your stay so you can experience this natural paradise responsibly.

At Russian Gulch, you will find something for everyone. Whether you desire a relaxing beach day or a hike along a rugged coastal trail, you will find it here. Don't miss out on this unique park and all its attractions. Enjoy the breathtaking views and make tons of memories in Russian Gulch State Park.

## Big Basin Redwoods State Park

Big Basin Redwoods State Park, in the Santa Cruz Mountains of California, is one of the country's oldest and largest state parks. It's home to some of the oldest living things on Earth – trees taller than the Statue of Liberty, over 2000 years old. Experience nature at its finest while exploring this breathtaking park, with its towering redwood forests, lush valleys, and stunning waterfalls.

Several different campgrounds are available for tent and RV camping for camping out in Big Basin Redwoods State Park. Among them are Big Basin Redwoods Campground, with sites equipped with picnic tables, fire pits, hot showers, and flush toilets, and Sempervirens Campground, which offers a peaceful camping experience surrounded by ancient redwoods. Huckleberry Campground with sites situated along the scenic Skyline-to-the-Sea Trail.

Big Basin Redwoods State Park is packed with exploration opportunities. Take in the majestic views of towering old-growth redwood forests on the popular Redwood Loop Trail, or take a longer trek to Berry Creek Falls—a nine-mile round trip journey through meadows, ferns, and second-growth redwoods. Also, explore Rancho del Oso at the park's northern end – an area named after the former grizzly bear population. Wildlife like deer and coyotes can be spotted during hikes.

### *RV Camping Guidelines*

- All vehicles must be parked in designated campsites only.

- No vehicle over 25 feet is allowed on any campsite.

- Trailers are not allowed to remain at campsites while visitors explore.

- RV visitors to the park must secure a vehicle permit upon arrival with a valid registration and campground fee.

- Two tents or other temporary shade structures are allowed per site.

- Most sites located in the park offer full hookups.

- Generators must adhere to operating hours between 10 am and 8 pm. To ensure a pleasant experience for all campers, please observe 'Quiet Hours' after hours indicated on site signs each night.

- Campers anticipating a stay at Big Basin Redwoods State Park in the beautiful Santa Cruz Mountains should ensure they are aware of the park guidelines and regulations.

Big Basin Redwoods State Park has something for everyone, from self-guided strolls to longer hikes. Enjoy the unbeatable combination of ancient redwoods and breathtaking views this incredible park offers.

## Prairie Creek Redwoods State Park

Prairie Creek Redwoods State Park is located in the heart of California's Redwood Coast, about 25 miles north of Eureka. This park features lush second-growth redwood forests, wide open prairies, beautiful ocean beaches, and stunning fern-lined canyons. The campground at Prairie Creek offers numerous campsites for tent campers and RV owners; some sites have full hookups.

Major attractions in Prairie Creek include Fern Canyon, which features walls dripping with lush green ferns contrasting against the white sandstone canyon floor below. Other popular sites include Elk Prairie meadow and Gold Bluffs Beach; the latter stretches along 10 miles of wild Pacific coastline backed by sheer coastal bluffs.

Hiking trails in Prairie Creek also abound with options, like the Davison Trail and James Irvine Trail, which provide access to amazing redwood groves. The Newton B Drury Scenic Parkway is a popular drive offering scenic views of old-growth trees. The Prairie Creek Visitor Center features interactive exhibits about local wildlife and geological history.

### *RV Camping Guidelines*

When camping at Prairie Creek Redwoods State Park, it's important to abide by the park's rules and regulations.

- RV campers must have their vehicle registered with the state of California and an approved sanitation system.

- Pets are allowed in the campground but must be on a leash no longer than six feet long.

- All food products must be stored in approved containers to prevent wildlife from foraging.

- All campfires must be extinguished before leaving the campsite.

- Length restrictions for campground sites are a major concern for RVers, as all sites at the park are limited to 40 feet or less.

- All rigs must be self-contained and equipped with an approved sanitary disposal system. Generators are allowed but must be shut down by 10 pm each evening.

- Visitors should keep in mind that all sites are first come, first served – no reservations can be made ahead of time.

By taking a camping trip to Prairie Creek Redwoods State Park, you experience some of the best that Humboldt County offers: stunning views, old-growth forests, and miles of untouched coastline. Whether you're visiting as a family vacation or an adventure with friends, Prairie Creek offers something special for everyone. From exploring Fern Canyon to relaxing at Gold Bluffs Beach, this state park ensures wonderful memories – and photos – to last a lifetime.

## South Yuba River State Park

South Yuba River State Park lies in California's Sierra Foothills, a few hours east of Sacramento and west of Nevada City. The area is known for its spectacular river canyons, stunning waterfalls, and rolling hills, creating a tranquil backdrop for camping trips. Whether you want an adventure or merely to relax, South Yuba River offers something for everyone.

The park features two distinct campgrounds: Bridgeport, with RV hook-ups, and 49 Crossing, where tenting is allowed. Both offer access to some of the most beautiful sights in the region, including majestic rock formations along the riverbank, lush trails ideal for hiking and biking, and swimming holes perfect for cooling off on hot days.

Some major attractions and sights include picturesque waterfalls such as Indian Springs, the longest single-span covered bridge in the world, and dozens of historic sites related to California's gold rush. Several trails are nearby, including the Nevada City Trailhead providing access to miles of pristine wilderness, and Independence Trail, which follows a former Gold Rush era flume.

### *RV Camping Guidelines*

- RVers enjoying a camping experience at South Yuba River State Park must follow the park's rules and regulations.

- Maintain a safe distance from campfires.

- Keep pets leashed at all times.

- Disposing of the trash properly in designated areas.

- Fires outside designated fire rings are prohibited.

- No wood collecting is allowed.

Whether searching for a peaceful retreat or an exciting adventure, South Yuba River State Park offers something for everyone. With its stunning scenery, historic sites, and miles of trails to explore, this spot will make your camping trip a memorable one.

# Chapter 7

## North Carolina State Parks

Ｎorth Carolina State Parks usually see a large influx of visitors, mostly from the state's various regions or neighboring states. Foreign tourists visit the state parks occasionally.

The crowds are manageable, even after the persistent increase in attendance. Despite increased attendance, people can still go to state parks to relax in nature without bumping into others while taking photos. North Carolina has several well-known state parks, each with its unique attractions.

State parks are an excellent choice if you want to have a memorable vacation that will leave you reflecting on your experiences. In North Carolina's incredible state parks, you can plan various outdoor activities with your family. Independent adventures are available, including canoeing and sandboarding.

North Carolina state parks provide the adventure you seek, whether an all-day adventure or an evening spent under the stars. You can put your stamina to the test by climbing a beautiful peak or relaxing in a comfortable chair and taking in the sounds and sights of the tranquil lake and its relaxing waves. Most of the state's 41 parks have recreational centers and do not charge much for camping, horse stabling, or admission.

The following are some of North Carolina's most popular state parks, with their campsite guidelines:

## Carolina Beach State Park

Carolina Beach State Park, a party beach bank known as Pleasure Island, is a lovely 761-acre natural getaway from the attractions and activities on the Beach Boardwalk of Carolina. It is located 10 miles north of Wilmington city. Situated between the Cape Fear River and the Intracoastal Waterway, Carolina State Park is jointly managed by the U.S. Army and North Carolina.

Besides being located on a triangle of land, the name "Pleasure Island" refers to what Carolina residents can see in this state park. People flock to the shiny beach to see the diverse wildlife and experience the majesty of the native seagrasses and dunes.

The park contains many beautiful sights, including the Venus Flytrap and an amazing view of the Cape Fear River, the two main attractions. It's no secret that North Carolina's most beautiful natural plant life is found in the hiking trails of this popular campground. It features some of the state's largest collections of rare, natural carnivorous plant species, a marina, and unusual wildlife.

It's exciting to know that Carolina Beach State Park has nine designated hiking trails, and even more exciting to know these trails span seven miles. The hiking trails include the Oak toe trail, the Swamp trail, the Sand Live Oak trail, the Sugarloaf trail, the Flytrap trail, the Snow's Cut trail, the Fitness trail, and the Campground trail. Three trails connect to the Sugarloaf trail, and the Track trail connects to the Snow's Cut trail.

### *RV Camping Guidelines*

The campground has public facilities like bathhouses, restrooms, and barbecue pits. The majority of the campground sites are wheelchair accessible. The campgrounds have a few rules and guidelines for overnight camping. Below are some guidelines and information on this campsite.

- Carolina Beach State Park has 70 campsites without hookups and nine with full hookups, including electricity, water, and sewer. The park also has four camper lodges.

- Carolina Beach State Park is open all year for camping.

- Every campsite has a fire ring, a grill, and a picnic table.

- During holiday weekends, including Labor Day, Memorial Day, and the Fourth of July, you must stay for a minimum of two nights.

- Reservations can be made online. Reservations are strongly advised for camping at Carolina Beach State Park.

- Campers are expected to arrive near the gate before closing so they can easily enter their campsites before the gates close. The park gates are locked at specific closing times, depending on the season.

- The flushable water closet system, a dump site, drinkable water, coin-operated laundry infrastructure, a bathhouse, a marina store, and a marina, among other amenities, are available to campers.

## Chimney Rock State Park

Chimney Rock State Park in Rutherford County is an incredible 6,807-acre mountain park that can be reached from Asheville in under an hour. This State Park is well-known for Chimney Rock, the park's centerpiece and, of course, the source of its name. It has a 315-foot spire off the mountain that gives the impression of walking on a floating island.

Besides Chimney Rock, there are numerous incredible sights to see in Chimney Rock State Park. The park is well-known for its breathtaking scenery, including the 315-foot-tall Chimney Rock spire made of granite. It provides a stunning panoramic view of Hickory Nut Gorge and Lake Lure when accessed via an elevator.

Visitors are also drawn to the rare Devil's Head balancing rock, seen from the spire's top.

From the spire's peak, visitors are treated to a breathtaking panorama of the Chimney Rock community below and the thrilling sensation of flying over Hickory Nut Gorge. Other family-friendly attractions in Chimney Rock State Park include a public river walk along the park's riverbank and a miniature golf course. The park has six hiking trails, including a not-too-arduous route to the incredible 404-foot Hickory Nut Falls waterfall and a family-friendly nature walk.

The six hiking trails are the Hickory Nut Falls trail, the Great Woodland Adventure trail for kids, the Outcropping trail, the Skyline trail, the Four Seasons trail, and the Exclamation Point trail.

Although the park has no campsites, RV hookups, tent sites, and cabins are available for rent in the well-kept campgrounds. You can also camp nearby in Chimney Rock or approximately 5 miles down the road in Lake Lure. Lake James State Park is the closest State Park with a camping area.

### *RV Camping Guidelines*

- Chimney Rock campground has 16 campsites open all year and is equipped with vault toilets.

- It is a first-come, first-serve site with no reservations.

- An accessible fishing platform is located near the campground's entrance.

- Firewood in this camp contains insects and other pathogens that can harm the health of the western forest. Therefore, if you don't move firewood, you are doing your part to keep invasive species out of the forests of the Pacific Northwest. Rather, get and burn your firewood near your camping spot.

- The campground has running water.

- Use the leave-no-trace principle when engaging in recreational activities on public land.

## Jockey's Ridge State Park

Dare County, located on the Outer Banks, is home to Jockey's Ridge State Park. The park is popular because it has the tallest dune system on the Atlantic Coast and is an excellent spot to view sunsets and fly kites.

The park's towering dunes, which stand 80 to 100 feet tall, are the largest and most noticeable feature, as they appear to belong more in a vast desert than a coastal beach town. The dunes are barren, containing nothing but Outer Banks sand, providing an engaging playground for sand boarders, hang gliders, and anyone willing to take a long hike and admire some impressive island-spanning views.

Visitors to Jockey's Ridge State Park are permitted access through wetland habitats to kiteboarding, swimming, paddling, and surfing the wind on the Roanoke Sound trail. A private concessionaire offers gliding lessons, an official activity at Jockey's Ridge State Park. Other outdoor activities include kayaking, hiking, kiteboarding, basking in the sun, and other activities the entire family can enjoy at the diverse recreational center.

The park offers guests with mobility issues the opportunity to reserve an all-terrain vehicle to ride to the top of the dune. Near the park's entrance is an exhibit hall with detailed displays about the history of the infamous dunes and the wildlife visitors will encounter.

The Jockey's Ridge State Park features three separate trails, each one and a half miles long but suitable for a stroll with the family. These trails include the Track trail, the Roanoke Sound trail, and the Maritime Shrub trail. These three distinct trails are open to visitors, including birders, nature lovers, and hikers, at any time of year. The three trails meander through Jockey's Ridge State Park, providing various views of the park.

The Roanoke Sound trail provides a sound side beach easily accessible to visitors and includes land or water sports that an Outer Banks visitor or vacationer might find interesting. The track trail is a lengthy nature trail beginning near the visitor area and continues west of its dunes, tracing the shoreline of the Roanoke Sound trail before connecting to the Maritime Shrub trail.

Since Jockey's Ridge State Park is day-use-only, overnight camping is not permitted, but you can reserve a picnic shelter and hike in the dunes. It does not diminish that it is a Nags Head location certain to provide something for everyone and keep all crew members smiling and satisfactorily entertained.

## Crowders Mountain State Park

Crowders Mountain State Park, in Gaston County near Gastonia City, is a popular rock-climbing destination in North Carolina's south-central region. It is well-known for housing the Crowders Mountain peaks and the twin pinnacles. Crowders Mountain State Park takes pride in both mountains because they provide a breathtaking view of the surrounding Piedmont. The mountain rises approximately 1,625 feet (495 meters) above sea level.

The diversity and beauty of Crowders Mountain State Park are greatly appreciated by its miles of hiking trails. However, the courses offer rugged, towering cliffs and hikes. The park is home to a wide variety of resident birds, including predatory birds and songbirds, making it an excellent spot for birdwatching.

Rangers regularly provide educational and informative sessions about Crowders Mountain State Park.

Get in touch with the park's office if you'd like to book a guided tour of Crowders Mountain State Park for your club, class, or other gatherings.

Crowders Mountain State Park educational resources have been prepared for grades 5-7. They are aligned with North Carolina's competency-based curriculum in science, mathematics, and arts. Crowders Mountain educates students on fundamental geology topics like the rock cycle, weathering, and resource use. The program is accompanied by a teacher's guide and free training for educators.

Crowders Mountain's difficulty will appeal to experienced climbers. Climbing is only authorized in certain places. Pitons, bolts, and other similar items that can damage the cliff are not permitted. More information is available at the campground office.

The park requires all climbers to complete a climbing registration and activity permission, which can be obtained at the park office. This permission is free of charge. A permit duplicate must be turned in to the registration box or shown to a park ranger before any activity can begin. Participants are given an extra copy, which they must have when climbing.

Participant individuals are expected to take precautions for their safety, including getting the right education and gear and always acting appropriately. Standard rock-climbing precautions, including safety gear, must always be taken.

There are numerous hiking trails, including the Turnback trail, the Rocktop trail, the Fern trail, the Group Camping trail, the Ridgeline trail, the Lake trail, the Pinnacle trail, the Tower trail, the Backside trail, the Family Camping trail, and the Loop trail. On a clear day, several of these trails will lead you to Crowders Mountain's summit, where you can see the Charlotte skyscrapers in North Carolina.

The Ridgeline trail is difficult, and it connects to nearby National Military Parks and Kings Mountain State Park, providing access to the Pinnacle. Visitors love the challenging hikes on the park's many public trails, especially the Backside and Crowders trails up to

Crowders Mountain's peak, where they can see Charlotte's skyline from 25 miles.

Other attractions in Crowders Mountain State Park include a 9-acre lake with fishing opportunities, boat and canoe rentals, and Backcountry campsites only accessible with a permit.

### *RV Camping Guidelines*

- Water is available.

- Pit toilets are located nearby.

- Each of the six group sites can accommodate a maximum of 15 people.

- Larger groups can enjoy fellowship in the group camping arena.

- There is a small charge.

- Reservations must be made in advance.

## Cliffs of the Neuse State Park

Located in Pamlico County, the 1,094-acre Cliffs of the Neuse State Park is home to more than 420 native trees and plants. It offers breathtaking views of the 275-mile-long Neuse River, the state's longest river, which winds through Piedmont and eventually empties into the Pamlico Sound. A layer of seashells, gravel, shale, clay, and sand forms a rainbow of colors on the cliff face.

Animals like prothonotary warblers, river otters, northern parulas, and various nonvenomous snakes abound. During the summer, visitors to the park can enjoy an 11-acre swimming lake.

The best place to start your adventure is at the visitor's center, where you can learn about the area's cultural and environmental history. You can visit the Cliffs of the Neuse State Park museum, which features exhibits on the area's important ecological and geological history. The Park offers daily interactive sessions to supplement the museum tour.

The park's recreation activities center around an 11-acre artificial lake with a sandy beach, leaping platform, roped-off perimeter, bathhouse, and everything required for a relaxing swim.

Spots to cast a line while taking in the scenery are plenty along the banks of the Neuse. Bluegill, largemouth bass, and many catfish live in the river and its tributaries. White and hickory shad travel up the river in the spring. A state fishing license is necessary, and all Wildlife Resources Commission laws are strictly enforced.

The park's five hiking trails wind through various forest ecosystems and end at some of the best fishing spots along the river. From the museum's parking lot, you can access four of these trails; each is less than one mile long and provides a closer look into the heart of the Cliffs of the Neuse State Park.

Camping sites are available for guests to stay the night. The park's campground facility has 32 sites, three rental lodges, and a large campground for families. The Spanish Moss trail leads to the group camping area, while the family campsite is in a wooded area near the park's office. In addition, the Cliffs of the Neuse State Park offers tent and RV camping.

### *RV Camping Guidelines*

- The family campground is open from March 15th to November 30th.

- Each campsite has a grill, a fire pit, and picnic tables.

- Organized groups are given a section of the park to use for primitive camping.

- You must make a reservation to use the group camping site, which is open all year.

- Drinking water is available nearby.

- Washrooms, electricity, hot showers, and water are available throughout the campsite, with electricity located centrally.

- There are no electricity or water hookups at the family campsite, but there is a dump station.

- A family of six only can occupy a site.

- The park gates are closed at the designated closing hours, and campers are not permitted to leave after the park has closed or before 8 am, except for a medical emergency.

## Goose Creek State Park

Located south of Beaufort, South Carolina, on US-265, Goose Creek State Park is a beautiful 1.672-acre Park with a primitive campground, visitor center, and historical exhibits. Goose Creek State Park is located near the Pamlico Sound and is a fantastic park for tourism in Washington, where the hummingbird season makes it an even more appealing tourist destination.

Visitors to Goose Creek State Park are drawn to the Long Boardwalk, which leads to Blackbeard's Old Stomping Grounds. Huge plant life, like loblolly pine trees and waterfront, live oak, thrive. You will see palmettos and experience an unrivaled swamp firsthand.

In this eight-mile stretch of public hiking trails, you'll see varieties of wildlife, including black bears, white-tailed deer, bobcats, and migratory and wading birds. Goose Creek State Park has nine trails: the Flatty Creek trail, the Goose Creek trail, the Tar Kiln trail, the Huckleberry trail, the Easy Scenic trail, the Live Oak trail, the Palmetto Boardwalk trail, the Mallard Creek trail, and the Ivey Gut trail.

It is a primitive campground with 12 tent sites, so overnight camping is permitted. Goose Creek State Park has two camping areas: a primitive tent campground between the Flatty Creek and Goose Creek trails and a newly established loop with RV cabins and campsites. The RV camping area has 22 sites, each with full hookups (water, electricity, and sewer), and one is wheelchair accessible.

### *RV Camping Guidelines*
Each campsite includes a picnic table, a tent pad, a fire ring with a grill, a bathhouse near the loop entrance, and a lantern hook. Rules

and guidelines govern the Goose Creek State Park RV camping areas. These guidelines are as follows:

- The minimum check-in age is 18 years.

- Check-in begins at 2 pm.

- Check-out time starts at 1 pm.

- Pets are permitted in the camping area.

- You must contact the Reservation Department to make arrangements for late arrival.

- Guests and visitors aged 12 and under are considered children at check-in time.

- The displayed camping rates do not include incidental charges or applicable service bills.

North Carolina is home to a diverse range of ancient mountains. Many have been transformed into beautiful tumbling monadnock hills, including cleverly carved rock formations, making the state parks ideal for camping and hiking trips. It would be best to contact the parks ahead of time to confirm their current hours of operation.

North Carolina's state parks are the best places to experience the state's breathtaking natural features, indulge in your favorite outdoor activities, and learn about the state's fascinating culture, science, and history.

# Chapter 8

## Montana State Parks

Montana is a beautiful state known for its incredible landscapes and vast wilderness. With so much to explore, it's no wonder there are many world-class parks in the state. Montana is full of spectacular outdoor adventures waiting to be explored. For those looking for something a little more accessible than the national parks, Montana State Parks offer an array of activities and stunning landscapes that can't be found anywhere else.

Camping is one of the most popular activities in Montana, with many camping spots to choose from. You can camp at tent sites and RV parks with full hookups or go into the wilderness and stay at primitive dispersed camping sites. These camping spots are located near towns and cities, down miles of dirt roads, close to fishing lakes and rivers, and in national parks. No matter which part of Montana you wish to explore, a great camping spot will await you.

This chapter overviews Montana's most popular state parks and discusses their activities and RV camping guidelines.

## Yellowstone Grizzly State Park

It is one of Montana's most popular state parks. Located close to the entrance of Yellowstone National Park, Yellowstone Grizzly State Park offers a unique wildlife experience. As its name implies, this state park is known for its large population of grizzly bears. Visitors can spot these majestic creatures from designated viewing areas or on trails along the river. The park has camping sites for tents, RVs, and boat launch access. It is a full-service RV park located in the heart of Yellowstone Park. There are plenty of sights to enjoy, from wildlife to stunning views.

The park offers tent camping and RV camping. For the adventurer, the park offers several trails for hiking, biking, and horseback riding. Plenty of fishing opportunities are in the surrounding area.

Yellowstone Grizzly RV Park is a great place to take in the sights and sounds of nature. The park offers several stunning views, including spectacular mountain peaks, rolling hills, and meadows filled with wildflowers. Additionally, plenty of geysers and hot springs can be observed. In Yellowstone RV Park, you will encounter many species of wildlife, like deer, elk, and other wild animals frequently seen in the park. Grizzlies and wolves can be spotted from a distance. Practice bear safety when in the park, as they can be dangerous if provoked. The park is home to various birds, including eagles and hawks. Birdwatchers will thoroughly enjoy the sights and sounds of nature in this park.

For those looking for a more relaxed experience, Yellowstone Grizzly RV Park offers many amenities, such as showers, laundry facilities, and Wi-Fi access. The park allows visitors to bring their pets as long as they adhere to the rules and regulations.

Grizzly RV Park offers various activities. Visitors can explore the park's many hiking trails and picnic sites. The park is home to numerous rivers flowing with abundant fish; anglers will find plenty of trout and other species or take a leisurely boat ride. Nearby restaurants are available to get your supplies or enjoy a meal.

Yellowstone Grizzly RV Park is a great choice for a relaxing camping experience in the heart of Montana. The park offers stunning views, plenty of wildlife sightings, and a perfect spot to escape everyday issues and reconnect with nature.

### *RV Camping Guidelines*

Yellowstone Grizzly RV Park & Cabins is ideal for exploring Montana's natural beauty. Following the guidelines, RVing in Yellowstone National Park is a great experience.

- Know the size of your RV, including towed vehicles, before reserving a campsite.

- It is the only park campground that offers a full hookup. Other campgrounds have dumping stations but do not allow slide-outs or are not wide enough.

- All campgrounds in Yellowstone require size restrictions and are subject to bear activity.

- For the quickest access to park attractions, use the West or North Entrances, which have private RV parks nearby.

- Yellowstone has uneven RV sites. Always check with local authorities before camping in these areas.

State parks like Yellowstone National Park are popular in Montana for a good reason. With its wealth of outdoor activities, stunning scenery, and abundant wildlife, it's no wonder so many people choose to explore this incredible park. With RV camping regulations to protect the environment and ensure everyone has a great experience, there's no reason you shouldn't enjoy the beauty of Yellowstone National Park with your RV.

## Lewis and Clark Caverns State Park

It is located in eastern Montana and was first established as a national monument in 1908. Visitors to the Lewis and Clark Caverns State Park can enjoy various activities, including wildlife observation and hiking. The grounds are inhabited by coyotes, elk, various birds, and 11 bat species, which make their home in the caves. If you're traveling with kids, pick up Junior Ranger booklets at the Visitor's Center to learn interesting facts about wildlife, plants, and caves.

They can turn in their completed booklets at the center to receive a Junior Ranger badge or small prize. In-season, guided cave tours explore two miles of lighted caverns and take around two hours to complete. The tour includes 600 stairs, areas that require stooping, and some sliding.

There is a shortened tour for the less adventurous and an intense tour for adventurers seeking a greater challenge. Hikers can choose from over 10 miles of trails to explore, varying in difficulty from easy-level walks to more demanding hikes.

After a day of adventure, head back to the campground and take advantage of its 40 spacious campsites. With full hookups and an RV dump station, you can rest easy knowing you have everything for a comfortable stay. The restrooms are equipped with hot showers and flush toilets, so you can freshen up after a day of exploring. Make the most of your trip and camp in style.

### *RV Camping Guidelines*

- It's easily accessible from State Highway 2, and the campground is equipped with paved roads and level gravel areas for camping.

- Vehicles can park at the Visitors Center near the campground entrance. The road leading up to the caverns is quite steep and winding, making it difficult for larger RVs or trailers.

- Rattlesnakes inhabit the Lewis and Clark Caverns State Park, so RV campers should exercise caution when exploring the grounds.

- Remember, bats inhabit caves, so it's essential to take extra care not to disturb them or their habitat.

- When packing for your trip, bring an extra layer of clothing and hiking boots to make the most of the park.

With its diverse wildlife, scenic trails, and fascinating cave tours, Lewis and Clark Caverns State Park is an ideal destination for nature lovers.

## Salmon Lake State Park

For an outdoor adventure, Salmon Lake State Park is the perfect spot. Located between two of Montana's most majestic mountain ranges, the Mission and Swan Mountains, this park offers breathtaking views and plenty of outdoor activities. You can camp with family and friends or spend a day fishing in Clearwater River or Salmon Lake.

The lake is home to various fish species, including cutthroat and northern pike, brown trout, kokanee salmon, and white mountain whitefish. Bird watchers will be amazed at the array of birds in the area, such as red-necked grebes, bald eagles, great blue herons, and osprey.

The park offers electric hookups, firewood for sale, grills, fire rings, ADA-accessible facilities, a picnic shelter, showers, toilets, and bike maintenance stands. The hike-bike site has a fire ring, bicycle rack, bear-resistant food lockers, and a covered shelter with picnic tables.

Hours of operation vary depending on the season, but the park is open to visitors from May through October. During the winter months, it's only accessible by foot, so visitors can still enjoy the scenery and nature.

Salmon Lake State Park is the perfect destination for anyone exploring the great outdoors with their RV. It has 24 campsites, including a hike-bike site for up to 10 tents.

### *RV Camping Guidelines*

RV guidelines must be followed when visiting the Montana state parks to ensure an enjoyable stay:

- Campsites fees vary depending on the season and amenities, ranging from $4 to $34 per night.

- Swimming areas are marked with buoys indicating a designated area where swimming is permitted. It is prohibited for boats to operate closer than 100 feet to buoys.

- Public docks are only used for loading and unloading, not leaving boats unattended.

- Natural resources must not be damaged by cutting or destroying trees, shrubs, or plants. Disturbance of topsoil is prohibited.

- Visitors must refrain from creating excessive noise, like a barking dog, especially during quiet hours.

- Disobedience to these rules will result in park employees asking visitors to leave.

- Pack plenty of food and water for your pet, especially if camping overnight.

- Keep pets quiet and prevent them from digging or entering public buildings.

- Know the camping fees, which vary depending on season and amenities

- Pet owners must be responsible for properly removing and disposing of any waste from their pets.

## Columbia Falls RV Park

Columbia Falls RV Park is located in the beautiful Glacier Country region of Montana, making it a great spot for campers to access all Glacier National Park offers. The RV park boasts 76 sites with full hookups accommodating any size vehicle, with stunning mountain views and friendly office staff.

The national park is a magnificent 1 million-acre area of untouched wilderness, and it's easy to see why it attracts over 2 million visitors yearly. The stunning mountain views make this campground especially picturesque, and its proximity to nearby parks and attractions makes it even more appealing. Glacier National Park offers blooming wildflowers, abundant wildlife, and plenty of raging waterfalls and rivers during the summer months. For an even more unique experience, wintertime brings snow-covered trees and perfect trails for snowshoers and skiers.

Columbia Falls, the nearby town of around 4,800 year-round residents, is only 14 miles from the park's entrance. Visitors can enjoy outdoor activities such as fishing, river floats, hiking, cross-country skiing, and snowmobiling. Other attractions include the Big Sky Water Park, City Pool, Pinewood Park, and a bowling alley. These attractions combine to make Columbia Falls the perfect destination for an escape into nature while still having access to plenty of activities.

For those hungry who want to grab a bite, head to Backslope Brewing for craft beer and homemade meals or Three Forks Grille for Italian food with a Rocky Mountain twist. The Whitefish Farmers' Market and Columbia Falls Community Market are great spots to pick up fresh produce and locally-made items.

Campground staff at Columbia Falls RV Park strive to ensure visitors have a positive and safe experience. Campers should review the park's rules before their stay, as a violation of any rule can result in immediate removal from the park without a refund.

### *RV Camping Guidelines*

- Check-in time is 3 pm, and check-out time is 11 am.

- Amenities such as hookups for water, electricity, and sewerage for camping are in all RV parks.

- Always follow posted signs and obey the speed limit.

- Pets are welcome in the campsite but should be taken to the designated pet walk area for exercise.

- Visitors must be registered at the office before parking their vehicle in the designated visitor parking area.

- Wi-Fi is available for all guests, and vehicles are limited to one RV and one car or truck per site.

- The speed limit throughout the park is 5MPH, so watch your speed.

- Seasonal sites are available upon request and have different cancellation policies than daily reservations.

- Cancellations must be made 14 or more days before arrival for a full refund.

- Quiet hours are from 10 pm to 7 am.

- RV reservations require a deposit of your first night's stay charged to your credit card when booking. You must provide 48 hours notice to cancel daily reservations and pay a $20 cancellation fee. Weekly reservations require 10 days' notice and a $50 fee, while monthly bookings require 30 days' notice and incur a $100 charge for cancellations.

- If you want to guarantee your favorite site or cabin, you can pay the applicable locking fee when making your reservation.

There's something for everyone in Columbia Falls, from outdoor enthusiasts to simply seeking a quiet mountain retreat. The RV park provides all the necessary amenities to make your stay comfortable and enjoyable. The park has easy access to nearby attractions and nature-filled activities in Glacier National Park. With so much to offer, Columbia Falls RV Park is the perfect home away from home.

## Bearmouth Chalet Park

Bearmouth Chalet Park is a great destination for families to escape the hustle and bustle of everyday life. Situated on over 180 acres of a beautiful, tranquil landscape near Clinton, Montana, visitors can enjoy stunning sunsets while relaxing with their loved ones in this pet-friendly park.

Despite exploring the beauty of their surroundings, visitors can enjoy nearby attractions like Garnet Ghost Town and Phillipsburg. The park is centrally located in western Montana, making it easy to take day trips to fish, float, or bike. You'll find plenty of trails here. The lonesome pine trail is perfect for a leisurely stroll, while the steep switchbacks of the high ridge trails provide more of a challenge. There's something at Bearmouth Chalet Park to suit your skill level and interest, on-trail, or off-trail.

It is located midway between Yellowstone and Glacier National Parks and provides easy access to both. For a place to camp out with your RV, this is the place. Bearmouth Chalet and RV Park feature 46 RV sites, big rig friendly, and pull-thru sites with full hookups, dry tent sites, dump stations, water, laundry facilities, clean bathrooms with hot showers, and propane for sale. If tent camping is more your style, plenty of sites are available, too.

### *RV Camping Guidelines*

The park offers RV camping with plenty of rules and regulations. For safety reasons, all campers must ensure their RVs are in a safe place at all times.

- Fires should be contained to grills or fire pits, and no wood can be gathered in the park.

- Quiet hours are from 10 pm-7 am.

- All dumps must be done in designated areas.

- All pets must be kept on leashes to protect wildlife from the campsites.

- All speed limits must be adhered to for everyone's safety.

Bearmouth Chalet and RV Park truly offer something for everyone, from outdoor enthusiasts to nature lovers. With stunning scenery, convenient amenities, and plenty of trails for exploring, it's a perfect destination for an unforgettable camping experience.

## Big Arm State Park

A stunningly scenic lakefront state park, Big Arm is situated in Montana's Flathead Lake region. With its crystal clear waters, diverse wildlife, and a wide array of activities, it's a perfect destination for anyone who loves the great outdoors.

Big Arm State Park is a great destination for outdoor lovers. It features the large, natural Flathead Lake, which covers 15 miles in width and 28 miles in length. At an elevation of 3000 feet, the park has 217 acres with 70 campsites.

This state park offers something for everyone. Visitors can enjoy swimming, fishing, and boating in Flathead Lake or explore trails that wind through the area. In addition to its many natural attractions, Big Arm features an observation tower with views of the valley below and many picnic spots. It's home to some of the best birdwatching in the state.

Campers and hikers will find plenty to explore at Big Arm, with several campgrounds and trails ranging from easy to difficult, so there's a trail for everyone. For those looking for a challenge, bike trails offer scenic views and exhilarating rides.

For something a little different, Big Arm offers educational tours that provide insight into the local flora and fauna. Ranger-led excursions to discover aboriginal sites in the region are available.

Photographers will appreciate the area's nature scenes and numerous activities like boating, biking, hiking, and scuba diving. Nearby, Wild Horse Island State Park is a 2,100-acre island off Flathead Lake's west shore, providing habitat for bighorn sheep, bald eagles, and wild horses - only accessible by boat.

### RV Camping Guidelines

The Big Arm State Park has strict rules to protect the environment and ensure a safe and enjoyable experience for visitors.

- Park visitors must obtain a joint state and tribal fishing license for fishing
- RVs and trailers are limited to 30 feet in size
- Visiting the park with pets requires leashes
- Camping fees and day-use fees apply
- Stays are limited to 14 days within 30 days

- Yurts are available for rent and come with electricity, heat, lights, and a propane barbecue.

- Visitors must bring their own bedding, personal toiletries, cooking utensils, a flashlight, and a container for water.

- All visitors must follow guidelines for bear-resistant storage lockers when provided.

Big Arm State Park is an outdoor paradise and a must-see destination for unforgettable adventures. Whether you're a nature enthusiast, adrenaline-seeker, or merely looking for a place to relax and take in the beauty of the great outdoors, Big Arm has something for everyone.

Montana is home to spectacular state parks, each offering something unique and special. Whether looking for outdoor recreation activities like hiking, biking, and swimming, a peaceful spot to camp overnight, or linger in the sun, Montana's state parks are sure to please. Make sure you know and understand the guidelines and regulations before you go so you can plan ahead and enjoy a safe and enjoyable experience. Remember to take in the stunning views of Montana's breathtaking landscapes while you're there - it's an experience you will never forget.

# Chapter 9

## Florida State Parks

Are you up for a thrilling adventure? Is an isolated, distant island more your style? What about a land or water trail? Are you looking for a good swimming area? Or are you looking for a peaceful camping spot?

Florida's state park system offers all this and more, creating a unique outdoor experience.

The Sunshine State's wilds are appealing, with plenty for adventurers, ecotourists, dreamers, and history enthusiasts of all stripes to enjoy.

These natural theme parks, which span over 1,250 square miles, showcase the finest of the state's untapped natural treasures, including waterfalls, beaches, and fascinating caverns. The water in these springs is crystal clear.

Florida is home to almost two hundred parks, campsites, preserves, leisure zones, and trailheads. There's a place here for everyone.

However, why limit yourself to only one park? Get an Annual Pass to visit several. See the best ones below to get started.

### Silver Spring State Park

You will find Silver Spring State Park east of Ocala on State Road 35, a mile south of State Road 40. It is famous for its Glass Bottom Boat Tours.

This park has dozens of springs, more than ten separate ecological communities, and miles of spectacular trails. The park is home to the Silver River Museum and a pioneer cracker town.

Visitors can go canoeing down the glistening river, hiking or biking along the natural trails, or relax and observe the many bird species and other animals.

There is a playground for the kids and three pavilions with grills available for hire for large gatherings.

Ten opulent cabins at Silver River can accommodate up to six guests each. Each cabin is fully furnished with a kitchen, two bedrooms, a bath, gas stove, air conditioner, heater, screened porch, dining area, kitchen, linens, towels, tables, and rocking chairs. You only need to bring food and your belongings.

Both camping loops include accessible restrooms and shower locations. The picnic area also has a public bathroom.

Kids will enjoy a wonderful playground with a swing set and monkey bars next to the picnic area. In case of "spills," the ground is covered with a special rubber mat for a safe surface.

Grills, fans, tables, plugs, and running water are available in the three open-air pavilions that make up the picnic area. A playground for kids is also in this area. Contact the park to make a reservation for the pavilions.

Nearly 15 miles of bicycling and hiking trails weave through various environments around Silver River. The courses provide a view of the great range of habitats of Central Florida, from marsh and swamp to the pine forest.

The 15 miles of off-road bicycle trails are open to the public. While bicycling, remember these trails also have foot traffic.

The controlled burning, Florida black bear, and migrating birds are a few topics covered in the displays found at the kiosks located at most trailheads.

### RV Camping Guidelines

- The hours of operation at Silver Springs State Park are from 8 am to dusk every day of the year, including holidays and weekends.

- The entrance fee is $2. Children under the age of six are not charged.

- All flora, fauna, and park assets are safeguarded. It is forbidden to collect, destroy, or cause trouble.

- The campsite, picnic area, and hiking paths are pet-friendly. Pets must always be on leashes, and owners are responsible for cleaning up after them. Dogs are not allowed in toilets, restaurants, museum, teaching center, cabins, or other structures. Animals for assistance are permitted anywhere.

- The park has a no-fishing policy.

- Silver Springs is currently not open for swimming. Visitors can enjoy boating, kayaking, and canoeing to see the stunning waterways firsthand.

- The river is off-limits to tobacco products. Only non-disposable containers containing food and drink are allowed on the river.

- You are not allowed to drink alcohol.

- Fireworks are strictly forbidden.

## Myakka River State Park

Myakka River State Park, one of the biggest and oldest state parks, is located on State Road 72, 15 kilometers east of Sarasota. It safeguards one of the most diversified natural regions in the state. This park is famous for boating, fishing, canoeing, and kayaking activities.

A boardwalk over Upper Myakka Lake offers visitors a great vantage point for watching animals. Visitors can wander along the canopied path to see life in the trees.

Upper Myakka Lake is accessible by a boat launch. The park's river and two lakes provide good boating, fishing, and kayaking options. Large swaths of uncommon Florida dry grassland are accessible by hiking paths. The two biggest airboats in the world are available for scenic lake rides daily. Safari tram rides of the park's wilderness are available from the middle of December until the beginning of May.

Developed and undeveloped campsites are available. The Civilian Conservation Corps constructed five palm log cottages in the 1930s, which have been updated to provide excellent housing.

The Myakka Movies can be viewed at the park's visitor center, which displays exhibitions about local species and their environments.

Myakka Outpost offers a variety of goods for sale, including gator stew, sandwiches, ice cream, t-shirts, caps, field guides, and nature books. They provide kayaks, canoes, and bicycle rentals.

Five vintage log cottages with space for up to 6 guests and 76 campsites are available. All have access to power and water. A sewage-disposal site is close to the campsite in Old Prairie. Each campsite is about 40 yards from a bathroom with a hot shower.

A boat ramp can access Upper Myakka Lake. Along the main route, there are picnic places with additional canoe launch sites.

The park map and brochure specify picnic spaces with tables and grills. Pavilions can be rented but are first come, first served. A charge is required to book a pavilion.

Sign up in advance to ride the multi-looped, 14-mile trail with your horse. It is necessary to provide negative Coggins test documentation. The usage of the horse trail is subject to an extra charge. The trail is muddy and bug-filled in the summer and travels through marshes, grassland, and hammocks.

The Myakka River provides cyclists with a range of possibilities to experience the region's distinctive scenery. The park offers accessible nature programs and guided excursions.

### RV Camping Guidelines

- The park is open every day of the year from 8 am to dusk.

- Each visitor must pay a $6 admission charge.

- Many historical sites, tourist centers, and museums might be closed on Tuesday and Wednesday each week.

- Fireworks are not permitted.

- A few locations welcome pets.

## Jonathan Dickson State Park

South of Stuart lies the Jonathan Dickinson State Park, best known for its river. This park is home to a variety of animals in its 13 natural groups, including mangrove swamps, pine flatwoods, sand pine scrub, and river swamps. The Loxahatchee River, the state's first river to be designated by the federal government, flows through the park.

Bike paths, horse routes, and hiking trails are available for visitors. Another excellent method to explore the park is by boat, canoe, or kayak along the river. Anglers can cast a line from the bank of a river or a boat on a lake to catch freshwater fish. The park has two full-service campsites and a youth (or group) rustic campground. Canoe, kayak, and motorboat rentals are available, and visitors can schedule boat excursions on the river.

At Jonathan Dickinson State Park, visitors can see a wide variety of animals, including deer, raccoons, otters, and bobcats. Alligators and turtles are often seen near the river. Several animals native to Florida are at risk of extinction, including the scrub jay, gopher tortoise, and Eastern indigo snake. Jonathan Dickinson is a renowned birding site with over 140 bird species.

Start your visit to the park at the Elsa Kimbell Environmental Education and Research Center. Visitors can explore the park's natural and cultural features through interactive and educational exhibits.

A small selection of groceries, beverages, snacks, and souvenirs is available at the River Store, close to the picnic area. Canoes and motorboats rentals and tour boat tickets are available at the store. You also check in and out of your cabin at the store.

There are twelve rental cabins close to Loxahatchee with three distinct cabin types, and each is furnished with everything, including bed and shower linens. There are two family campsites in Jonathan Dickinson State Park. East of the park's ranger station is the Pine Grove Campground, which has 90 sites. The River Campground is located along the Loxahatchee River, six kilometers from the entrance, with 45 sites. Water, electricity, a picnic table, and a grill are available at each campsite. The bathrooms are spacious and well-tiled. Every campsite has a disposal station.

There is a lovely swimming beach with sand on the Loxahatchee River's beaches. Please be careful since there are no lifeguards on duty. It is next to the Loxahatchee picnic pavilion, which can be reserved, and a brand-new, contemporary restroom with an outdoor shower. To check the status of the swimming area, please contact the park.

An access point to an eight-mile trail system is near the Eaglesview area for those bringing their horses to the park on a trailer. The ranger station has trail maps for sale. There is a fully equipped, five-site campsite for horse owners to enjoy. Horses must be kept in robust portable enclosures or tied overnight to the designated timeout posts.

There are accessible paved and off-road bike routes. Paved pathways extend for nearly two miles following the former alignment of Old Dixie Highway. A nine-mile system of mountain biking trails is at Camp Murphy, ranging from easy to "black diamond, experts only."

## *RV Camping Guidelines*

- Florida State Parks are open daily from 8 am until sunset.

- Visitors must pay a $6 admission charge.

- The park's vegetation, animals, and property are all protected.

- Hunting is not permitted.

- Alcoholic beverages are only permitted in authorized places.

## Bahia Honda State Park

Bahia Honda lies 19 kilometers south of Marathon. This state park is well-known for its stunning beaches, breathtaking sunsets, and good snorkeling. Visitors can dine on the beach, swim, or relax and enjoy the year-round breezes that cuddle the coastlines. The park's concession rents kayaks and snorkeling equipment, and boat cruises to the reef are available for snorkeling expeditions. Anyone with a boat or desiring to fish from the shore can use the boat ramp.

Wading birds can be seen in abundance in Bahia Honda. The nature reserve teaches visitors about the island's distinctive vegetation and fauna. Full-service campsites and holiday cottages are available.

Three duplex cabins are outfitted with sleeping spaces for up to 6 persons in each cabin. Each cabin includes cooking equipment, utensils, and bedding. The cabins contain a complete bath, central air conditioning and heating, two bedrooms, and a living room space. Each cottage has a lofted porch and a ground-level wooden deck with a barbecue and outdoor seating. Reservations must be made 11 months in advance for the wintertime, weekends, and holidays.

There are several pavilions and a restroom with outside freshwater showers.

It's no surprise that boating is a favorite pastime in Bahia Honda, given its proximity to the Gulf of Mexico and the Atlantic Ocean.

There are numerous fishing spots in the park. Bottom fishing for snapper is possible off the ancient sea walls on each side of the Old Bahia Honda Bridge. The island's Atlantic side has shallow sand flats ideal for fly-fishing for bonefish and barracuda.

There are two nature trails in the park. You can pick up a self-guided booklet and visit the Silver Palm Trail at Sandspur, in the island's southeastern part. The second trail is on the island's southwestern edge in the Calusa region. It ascends to the Old Bahia Honda Bridge. From the bridge's highest point, you can take in a breathtaking panorama of the whole island. You can see the water below from above. You could observe huge rays or fish leaping. Sea turtles and fish can be seen swimming under the water's surface if it is clear. Several butterfly species will bless your eyes along the trail's edge.

## RV Camping Guidelines

- The parks are accessible daily from 8:00 am to dusk throughout the year.

- The park charges an $8 admission fee. Camping, kayak rentals, and excursions incur additional user costs.

- Fishing, boating, swimming, and burning are only permitted in defined places.

- Fireworks are not allowed.

- Consumption of alcohol is restricted to certain areas.

## Grayton Beach State Park

The Grayton Beach State Park is located south of U.S. 98 off of County Road 30A, close to the city of Grayton Beach. It is one of the United States' most stunning and unspoiled beaches. The beach is a beautiful place to swim, sunbathe, and go surf fishing. Visitors can get an up-close look at a salt marsh habitat by paddling a canoe or kayak on Western Lake.

Hikers and bikers can enjoy almost four miles of paths amid pine Flatwoods; the route starts across Highway 30-A from the park entrance. The coastal woodland the trail passes through is full of magnolias twisted and bent by the sea winds, giving them an unsettling "Middle Earth" appearance. Thanks to the boat ramp that leads right into the lake, you can fish in freshwater or saltwater.

Grayton Beach campsite is one of the most beautiful on the Gulf Coast. The woods and shrubbery separating the sites give the impression you are miles away from civilization, but with running water, electricity, and a toilet with hot showers. You can have a fantastic camping experience with your RV or tent.

Instead of living in an RV, you can stay in their duplex cabins. The cottages are secluded in the pine trees yet are a few minutes from the Gulf of Mexico. Six people can fit in a cabin. Grayton Beach State Park has thirty duplex cottages with two bedrooms and one bathroom. Cabin amenities include a gas fireplace (for use between November and March), cooling systems, a fully equipped kitchen, a screened-in porch, and an outside grill. All necessary linens, sheets, pillowcases, blankets, and towels are included. You only need to pack the basics, like coffee, filters, toilet paper, shampoo, and soap. A queen bed is in the front bedroom, while two (2) twin beds are in the rear bedroom of most cabins.

Take advantage of one of the world's most gorgeous beaches by lounging on the sugar sand and swimming in the emerald Gulf of Mexico. Also, don't miss out on a Grayton Beach sunset.

The beach trail starts at the parking area and goes through sand dunes and scrub ecosystems. A self-guiding pamphlet is provided to understand the trail.

Grayton's Amphitheater is next to the Campground. During the summer, instructive events organized by rangers are held on the lake peninsula.

### *RV Camping Guidelines*

- The park is open daily from 8 am until dusk.

- The park charges a $5 entry fee.

- Everything in the park, from trees to animals to buildings, is protected. It is illegal to harvest, destroy, or disrupt plants and animals.

- Hunting is not permitted. The state reserves provide special hunting seasons.

- Fireworks are not permitted.

## Three Rivers State Park

Three Rivers State Park is located on State Road 271, two miles north of Sneads. The Chattahoochee and Flint rivers meet in southwest Georgia to create Lake Seminole, the backdrop for this serene park.

Hikers in these pine- and mixed hardwood-covered slopes will see squirrels, deer, foxes, and several resident and migratory bird species. Some of the State's best freshwater can be found here, and campers can fish from a pier 100 feet long or launch their boats from a boat ramp. A shaded picnic area overlooks the lake with tables and grills.

A picnic pavilion with seating for up to 60 persons can be rented for large gatherings. Overnight guests can stay in a full-service campsite near the lake or a contemporary cabin.

Three Rivers State Park has plenty of wildlife and birdwatching options. Bald Eagles can be seen flying over the lake, and they nest in the park.

Hundreds of waterfowl take shelter in the park's tranquil bays and sloughs. These squirrels are stunning, with silvery white hair and a black mask concealing their faces. Deer are often seen, as are raccoons and a colony of fox squirrels. Several unique or unusual plant species can be discovered in the park.

Thirty gorgeous, semi-private, and shaded campsites with water and electricity are available for reserve at the Lakeside Camping Area. From the campsites, you can see Florida and Georgia. There is a disposal station close to the camping area.

The park campsite has one cabin. The log cabin was constructed with modern conveniences, including central heating, air conditioning, and a cozy fireplace. A queen-sized bed is in one of the bedrooms on the first floor, and two twin-sized beds are in the little loft. The kitchen has everything for cooking, including an electric burner, a microwave, a fridge, and cooking utensils. The cabin has a fully functional bathroom with a shower. Don't forget to pack towels, sheets, food, and fishing equipment for a relaxing and enjoyable stay.

Given Lake Seminole's famed catches, fishing is a common pastime for park visitors. Anglers can reel in a wide variety of species, including largemouth bass, bluegill, and bream. Anyone over 16 in Florida must have a valid fishing license to fish in freshwater.

Canoeing and kayaking are popular activities on Lake Seminole. The park charges $12 per day for its aluminum canoes. Life jackets and paddles are available.

The park has 30 family sites ranging in size, and all have access to running water and electricity. The park has a disposal station. There is only one cottage for rent. There are three pavilions in the vast picnic area, each with picnic tables, barbecues, and neighboring bathrooms. There is also a group camp inside the park that can host up to a hundred tent campers.

The park has two hiking trails. One trail starts inside the campsite and takes guests on a picturesque walk along Lake Seminole's shores. The second trail begins at the picnic areas. It leads visitors on a challenging trek through the hilly terrain of this particular Florida region.

### RV Camping Guidelines

- Three Rivers State Park is open daily from 8 am until sunset.

- The park charges a $3 entry fee.

- Camping, canoe rentals, and excursions incur additional expenses.

- Pets are only allowed in certain places. Service animals are accepted in all parts of the parks.

- Fishing, boating, swimming, and burning are only permitted in defined places.

- A Florida state fishing license is necessary.

- Fireworks are not permitted.

- Hunting is not permitted.

Florida's state park system fosters and promotes a culture of inclusivity, equal access, and boundless opportunity to enjoy the beautiful nature in the Sunshine State. You can find parks with accessible amenities and activities in every state region.

# Chapter 10

# RV Maintenance and Problems to Avoid

▚▐◆▐▚▐◆▚▐◆▚▐◆▚▐▚◆▚◆▚◆▐▚◆▚▐▚◆▐

Maintaining your RV and its components is crucial if you want to enjoy a pleasurable camping trip. While RV camping is a truly fantastic experience, it comes with unexpected mishaps. This chapter explores common RV mistakes, maintenance tips, and relevant information to better plan your trip.

## Common Mistakes to Avoid

- Failing to check the weather stripping and sealants on your vehicle's windows. You can apply the self-adhesive weather stripping yourself if you find it damaged or worn out. A damaged weather stripping will result in poor temperature control inside the RV during camping.

- Avoid using the RV refrigerator like a regular freezer at home. Don't fill the fridge with food items; only pack the essentials. Furthermore, park the RV on flat terrain, as parking on an incline will affect the proper functionality of the refrigerator.

- Check the RV's roof for damage, as extreme weather conditions like heat, heavy rain, or snow can make the trip unpleasant. Several roof sealants can be applied to your RV's roof.

- Check the RV's interior for water damage before camping, as the cracks and seams can worsen.

- Conduct a thorough RV inspection before moving, and ensure the stairs are folded up and secured and the window vents are closed. Then check the oil, fuel levels, lights, generator, air filters, transmission fluids, and everything else. It will take some time to inspect, but it will ensure your RV stays in excellent condition while on a trip.

- Check the tires and ensure they are well-inflated at the correct pressure for the road. Inspect the spare tire to ensure it's in good condition. However, if you are still determining the condition of your tires, visit a tire professional to know if they are good to go or need replacing.

- Check the RV's batteries and ensure they are fully charged and functional. A battery typically lasts 3 to 5 years. After this period, the battery starts losing its efficiency. Therefore, replace or fully charge your battery before hitting the road.

- The water systems in your RV are gray water and black water tank systems. Each system must be cleaned with a specific cleaning chemical. Avoid using other chemicals, or it will result in an excessive buildup that will ultimately clog the system.

- Inspect your RV's braking system and ensure braking fluids are at optimum levels. If the brake shoes are worn, replacing them would be feasible before starting your RV camping trip.

- When towing the RV, check the electrical connection from your RV to the vehicle is working correctly.

- Avoid overloading the RV as it increases the chances of the RV flipping over during transportation. When packing, ensure heavy objects are placed low and light things are stacked on top. If you need help with what to pack and what to leave behind, consider making an RV items checklist to take advantage of all traveling essentials.

- Unlike regular toilet paper, specialized tissue paper is used in RV toilets. The toilet paper is 100% biodegradable and prevents clogging of the sewage system. Using regular toilet paper will eventually result in a clogged tank or pipeline during the trip.

Now that we've covered some common mistakes to avoid when planning an RV camping trip, let's dig deep to learn other maintenance tips and guidelines to enjoy your trip safely and without hassle.

## Hooking and Unhooking Your RV

Here is a thorough explanation of how to hook up and unhook an RV and advice on how to make the experience more pleasurable and straightforward.

Before you start, make sure you have all the necessary tools, such as your hitch, hitch ball, safety chains, electrical and water hoses, and additional adapters or attachments.

- Ensure adequate room for the hitch to connect and the RV to pass over any obstructions when positioning the RV in front of the tow vehicle.

- To anchor the RV in place, lower the stabilizing jacks and chocks.

- First, fasten the safety chains to the tow vehicle's bumper and the frame of the RV. These are crucial for extra stability and security if the hitch disconnects while you are driving.

- Connect the water and electrical hoses to the tow vehicle's connectors and the RV's utilities. This enables the RV to be powered and supplied with water while being transported.

- The hitch must now be connected. Locate the hitch receiver on the towing vehicle and the hitch ball on the RV. Place them so that the ball fits snugly into the receiver.

- Use the locking pin to fasten the hitch ball to the receiver after installing it. Ensure the hitch is tightened, and the locking pin is firmly engaged to guarantee a secure connection.

- Lastly, raise the stabilizing jacks and chocks on the RV and let go of the brakes. You are now prepared to travel.

Simply follow the same steps in reverse to unhitch the RV: lower the stabilizing jacks and chocks, cut the water and electricity hoses, release the locking pin, and remove the hitch ball. Always take your time and double-check your connections to ensure a safe and easy voyage.

## Emptying the RV Water Tanks

Regardless of the water system of your RV, emptying it is necessary when you want to store your RV or when going on a trip. Typically, the black water tank contains sewage water and should be emptied first, followed by opening the gray tank and using the water to rinse the sewer hole. Thoroughly wash the black tank with a pressure washer or a tank wand, and never leave any leftover water. When the tank is clean, you'll be able to see the sewer adapter.

After emptying the tank and flushing out all water, fill the bottom with two liters of clean water. Now treat the black water tank with a holding tank treatment of your preference to ensure the tank is clean. Don't forget to read the manufacturer's instructions to ensure the tank is cleaned correctly. The gray tank in your RV collects water from the RV sinks and showers. You can use a dishwashing liquid mixed with water or a treatment chemical to remove the grease and dirt buildup. Lastly, apply valve lubricants to your RV tank's valves to maintain their proper functioning.

When emptying the tanks, ensure you have the right tools like an RV sewer hose, clean sewer hose, disposable rubber gloves, elbow fitting, RV tank treatment chemicals, and a high-pressure washer. Here are step-wise instructions you can follow to empty the tanks:

1. Close the tank valves before you begin the cleaning operation.

2. Remove the sewer cap from the discharge port and attach one end of the hose with a sewer adapter. Then attach the other end with the discharge port.

3. Guide the hose to the sewer hole and use an elbow fitting to ensure the hose remains secured.

4. Open the black tank valve and let the water discharge into the sewer hole.

5. Similarly, open the gray tank valve to remove residual water.

6. Wait until the water is completely flushed, then remove the hoses and attachments.

7. Treat with a treatment chemical of your choice.

## Parking Your RV

Survey the parking space to identify a feasible spot. Drive your vehicle toward the spot and take your time when parking. If you are backing in, use your side and rearview mirrors to guide you in parking the RV in place. Avoid turning your steering wheel too much and go slowly when parking the vehicle. Once the RV is parked, check whether the RV is stable and not in an inclined position. A minor instability can result in poor sleep and make using the RV challenging. Some recent RV models have auto stabilization features that automatically adjust the level using hydraulics. However, if you don't have a system like this, don't worry and use the manual method.

You need several wood blocks, a bubble level, and wheel chocks. Place wheel chocks on the RV wheels to lock them in place. Then use your bubble level to find the area where you might need to adjust the level. Place wooden blocks below or near the wheels to adjust the level.

After leveling, you need to stabilize the RV. Your RV will have built-in stabilizer jacks in the frame, or you might have to add manual stabilizer jacks between the ground and the vehicle's frame. Even if the RV has built-in jacks, it's best to add a few stabilizer jacks manually, as it decreases the pressure on each jack.

## Turning on Your RV Water Heating System

Your RV has either a propane gas heater or an electric heater. While starting an eclectic water heater is just filling the heater water tank and turning on the switch to heat the water, propane gas takes much more preparation. Here's how you can start a propane gas water heater:

1. Fill up the water heater tank using a water hose and close the inlet valve after the tank is filled. If you are alone or don't want to heat a full tank, consider filling the tank halfway to save gas and water.

2. Close the heater bypass valve that typically directs water away from the heater. After closing the bypass valve, turn the hot water tap to see whether the water is flowing. You'll hear bubbling sounds and air coming out of the tap for a few seconds. Once the air is removed, water will start flowing, confirming the tank is leakproof and the heating system is working perfectly.

3. Locate the propane tank on your RV and see if it has an automatic or manual start. For the automatic start option, you only have to turn the water heater switch on and wait for the water to heat up. However, if there is a manual system, you must turn the gas on and rotate the knob from off to pilot. Now, ignite the pilot flame and wait at least 30 seconds to a minute. After a minute, turn the knob from the pilot to on to start the propane gas heater.

On average, electric and propane gas heaters take around 20 to 40 minutes to heat the water.

## Turning on Your RV Generator

While most campgrounds in state parks provide electrical hookups for your RV, there are several remote campsites where providing these amenities is nearly impossible. The first thing to do is select the right generator for your RV. Generators have different power outputs with varying dimensions. Always purchase a generator that fits in well with your RV dimensions and provides the required amperage, voltage, and wattage to keep your RV batteries charged and appliances running. Let's review how you'll be using the RV generator to generate electricity.

- Start by reading the instructions manual, as different generator models have slightly varying methods to operate them.

- Before starting the generator, ensure the appliances in your RV are turned off.

- Access the control panel in your RV and prime the generator fuel system by pressing down the stop button for a few seconds.

- Most generators use battery ignition and won't cause an issue when starting the generator.

- After the generator starts, keep it running for at least two minutes before putting in an electrical load.

## RV Generator Maintenance Tips

- Keep the generator clean at all times and prevent grime and dust from accumulating on the generator body.

- Ensure the exhaust pipe is away from the RV and open to prevent the engine from choking.

- Install a running hour meter to know when you need to change the generator engine oil for optimum performance.

- Avoid putting too much load for extended periods or operate the generator without putting any load.

## Using Your RV Awning

It's one of the best additions to your RV trailer as it can make any space shaded and comfy to enjoy and relish, especially when out camping. Let's read about how to set up your awning:

1. Loosen the rafter knobs on the support arms to release the awning. Some RVs have screws that can be removed when you need to use the awning and tighten them when traveling.

2. Squeeze the travel locks to release the support arms. You'll hear a clicking sound, confirming the travel locks are removed.

3. Change the position of the ratchet mechanism, allowing the awning to roll down slowly. You can use the awning rod to adjust the awning in place.

4. Using the awning rod, pull the strap holding the awning to extend it fully.

5. Slide the rafter arms to the desired angle and lock them to keep the awning in place.

6. Tighten the rafter knobs to ensure the awning arms and the fabric remain tight.

7. Now, raise the awning to the desired height. If you are doing it alone, increase the height on each arm a few inches at one time and switch between arms. Raising the awning with two people is comparatively easier as both arms can be increased in height simultaneously.

8. Lastly, check that the structure is sturdy and that no loose knobs or screws could damage the awning during high winds.

## Internet Access in Your RV

Nowadays, it's more accessible than ever to stay connected to the internet anywhere worldwide. You can use your phone's internet connection to provide internet access throughout the trip. However, a wireless internet modem would suffice if you wanted to have a movie night out while camping and streaming movies. Connect the dongle to your electronic devices to enjoy your internet. Most state parks also provide WiFi services in their campgrounds so that you won't have internet access issues.

## Toilet Usage Tips When Camping

- Understand the water controls of the installed toilet so you don't have to struggle afterward.

- Fill the toilet bowl a quarter with water before using the lavatory.

- Only use RV-friendly toilet paper that degrades quicker than regular toilet paper, reducing the chances of clogging.

- Avoid flushing anything other than the RV toilet paper into the water collection tanks.

- Regularly clean the toilet with a mild cleaner and disinfectant.

- Keep the ball valve seal lubricated for proper drainage.

## Disposing of Garbage When Camping

- Choose food items with less plastic packaging and opt for reusable containers for food items like meats, vegetables, and fruits. You can opt for biodegradable bags if available.

- Rinse the dishes well to leave no food smell on the plates.

- Keep leftover food in air-tight containers in the RV or outside the RV. Keeping the food in air-tight containers is necessary to prevent attracting animals to the RV.

- If you plan to stay for a few days, prepare a compost bin to dispose of vegetable and fruit waste, turning it into a biodegradable and organic fertilizer. Purchase a compost bin, as these bins are specifically made to keep the smell at bay.

- Never throw plastic waste and other garbage out in the wild. It's everyone's responsibility to keep these parks clean. Therefore, collect these waste materials in a large container and drop them off at a recycling point when returning home.

## Using a Propane Gas Oven

You'll be lighting up the stove using an automatic spark ignition or manually using a lighter or a match to start the flame. Turn the propane gas knob running to the stove. Push the knob on the stove and start the gas flow while igniting it with another flame.

## Leaving the Campgrounds

Whether it's the campsite's checkout time or the excitement of heading back home from your RV camping trip making you leave in a hurry, it's best to review the following steps to ensure you reach home safely.

- Anything outside your RV, including chairs, ropes, mats, rugs, entertainment systems, etc., is back in place.

- Empty your RV tanks, rinse them well, and rinse the sewer hoses before putting them away.

- Emptying fresh water tank supplies can save you fuel but keeping a small reserve would be a wise move in case of an emergency.

- Turn off the propane gas supply knob, disconnect the electrical hookup, and lock the access door.

- Check every storage or cargo door and ensure they don't remain open.

- Check the inflation in the RV tires and look for cracks.

- Check the coolant, brake fluid, and battery levels.

- When storing contents in your RV, ensure they are spread across properly to maintain balance while driving.

- Inspect the bathroom and check if the cabinets are closed, the shower sliders are locked in place, and the toilet door is latched to keep it in place.

- Wash, rinse, and dry your dishes before hitting the road and keep them in a secure container for better transportation. Stackable containers are a feasible choice for easy transportation of your dinnerware.

- Securely fasten countertop RV items, like your coffee maker or the TV, in place. Velcro is a sturdier option than magnetic latches and can be installed easily to prevent cabinet doors and drawers from opening while on the road.

- Pull in the slide-outs using a hand crank or push a button to let the mechanical motor work its magic.

- Retract the awning as you extend it, and ensure the locks are placed to keep it from opening.

- Retract automatic stabilizer jacks or remove manually placed stabilizers one at a time.

- Remove the wooden blocks from the tires and the wheel stoppers to allow the tires to move freely when towing.

Following this checklist will ensure your trip stays enjoyable and entertaining regardless of the RV you own. The information we provided in this chapter will keep your RV in good shape all year, reducing hefty repair bills and ensuring you don't have to deal with malfunctions or issues that might affect your trip.

Get the family or your companions involved when hooking up and unhooking your RV. Many hands make light work, creating a sense of unity, excitement, and achievement when it is done together. If your children are very young, let them help with packing the small items away that must be stored on ground level. Instead of them getting under your feet, they can contribute to the excitement.

# Conclusion

⊐▣◁◖⊂⊐▷◖⊂⊐▷◁◖⊂●◆◁◖⊂▷◁◖⊂

You know now that this book is a comprehensive guide to the best road trips in the United States. It is suitable for novices, easy to read, and, most importantly, contains step-by-step instructions and practical advice.

Planning and budgeting are key to RV camping. Planning gives you a framework for executing your financial goals, activities, travel seasons, and budgeting. It determines whether your strategy needs refining or expanding. You will encounter difficulties if you pack too much or too little, and if you pack enough but forget the essentials, you'll also have problems.

What is a road trip in your recreational vehicle if it does not operate properly and is not in good condition to ensure your safety? Before embarking on your trip, service your RV and, if possible, replace all the tires. How you drive significantly impacts how enjoyable your trip will be. Observing traffic laws and regulations, knowing when to enter and exit the roadway, avoiding rash decisions, and driving at a moderate speed are all necessary to ensure a safe and pleasant journey.

Your RV is your campsite and should always be kept clean. Hence, your food is safe, and the risk of becoming infected, sick, or bitten by insects is greatly reduced.

The United States of America is a beautiful country with a wealth of natural resources and various recreational activities available in its parks. Every park has something distinctive that would confuse you, but your interests and location determine which park you should visit first and when to see others.

Arizona, Wyoming, Washington, California, North Carolina, Montana, and Florida have amazing parks. Each state park has hiking trails and RV camping guides; you shouldn't deviate from them. Before you set out on your journey, a few skills are absolutely necessary for you to have mastered. Emptying tanks, turning on your generator, dealing with RV toilets, and packing up your RV to leave, are among several topics covered in the final chapter of this book.

Check the availability of each park you plan to visit, associated booking, entrance fee, and free day policies before you start your journey. Also, before buying souvenirs or packing any non-essential tools, consider whether or not you need them.

RV camping is not merely a holiday or a few days on the road; it is an adventure of a lifetime with those you love. We wish you safe travels and a thoroughly enjoyable trip.

Thank you for buying and reading/listening to our book. If you found this book useful/helpful, please take a few minutes and leave a review on Amazon.com or Audible.com (if you bought the audio version).

# References

Wendland, M. (2021, May 9). How to budget for RV travel to national parks. RV Lifestyle. https://rvlifestyle.com/how-to-budget-for-rv-travel-to-national-parks/

Bram. (2019, February 22). How to select which National Park to visit first? The National Parks Experience. https://www.travel-experience-live.com/how-select-first-national-park-visit-first/

Gulati, P. (2021, November 5). How to plan A trip in 5 simple steps. Traveltriangle.com. https://traveltriangle.com/blog/how-to-plan-a-trip/

What is Budgeting, and Why is it Important? (n.d.). My Money Coach. https://www.mymoneycoach.ca/budgeting/what-is-a-budget-planning-forecasting

10 RV camping essentials you absolutely must pack for your road trip. (2018, May 31). Adventure KT. https://adventurekt.com/rv-camping-essentials/

Gingerich, A. (2014, June 2). Ultimate RV packing list for a first-time camper. Campersinn.com. https://blog.campersinn.com/blog/ultimate-rv-packing-list-for-a-first-time-camper?hs_amp=true

Lawrence, E. (2021, September 25). 8 RV driving tips that can save your life. RV LIFE. https://rvlife.com/rv-driving-tips/

RV maintenance: 8 tips to prep your RV for the road. (2021, March 9). Geico.com; GEICO Living. https://www.geico.com/living/driving/rv-boat-more/spring-maintenance-for-your-rv/amp/

RVgeeks. (2022, June 20). RV driving tips: 21 ways to stay safe & calm. TheRVgeeks. https://www.thervgeeks.com/rv-driving/

Togo, R. V. (2021, April 12). How to pack your RV for a camping trip. Togo RV. https://togorv.com/rv-living/how-to-pack-your-rv/

Arizona state parks & trails. (n.d.). Azstateparks.com. https://azstateparks.com/

National & State Park guides. (n.d.). Outdoorsy. https://www.outdoorsy.com/guide/parks

Patagonia lake State Park in Arizona. (n.d.). Azstateparks.com. https://azstateparks.com/patagonia-lake

Swartz, N. P. (2019, October 1). All the best RV camping in Arizona national forests. Campendium. https://go.campendium.com/all-the-best-rv-camping-in-arizona-national-forests/

The best state parks in Arizona with RV camping. (n.d.). Cruiseamerica.com. https://www.cruiseamerica.com/rv-adventures/rv-destinations/rv-camping-in-arizona

Walker, T. (n.d.). List of parks in Arizona. Stateparks.com. https://stateparks.com/arizona_parks_and_recreation_destin ations.html

11 best national & state parks in Wyoming. (n.d.). Touropiahttps://www.touropia.com/best-national-state-parks-in-wyoming/

Ochs, A. (n.d.). The top state & national parks to check out in Wyoming. Trips To Discoverhttps://www.tripstodiscover.com/top-state-and-national-parks-in-wyoming/

Request Rejected. (n.d.). Wyo.govhttps://wyoparks.wyo.gov/

The best state parks in Wyoming: hot springs, cool lakes, and incredible views. (n.d.). Lonely Planethttps://www.lonelyplanet.com/articles/best-state-parks-wyoming

Walker, T. (n.d.-b). Buffalo Bill State Park. State Parkshttps://stateparks.com/buffalo_bill_state_park_in_wyo ming.html

Walker, T. (n.d.-c). Grand Teton National Park. State Parkshttps://stateparks.com/grand_teton_national_park_in_ wyoming.html

Walker, T. (n.d.-d). Yellowstone National Park. State Parkshttps://stateparks.com/yellowstone_national_park_in_ wyoming.html

Camping at Edness K. wilkins State Park. (n.d.).
Campnab.comhttps://campnab.com/parks/wyoming/edness-
k.-wilkins-state-park

Glendo State Park. (n.d.).
Outdoorsyhttps://www.outdoorsy.com/guide/glendo-state-
park-wy

(N.d.).
Tripadvisor.comhttps://www.tripadvisor.com/Hotel_Review
-g60472-d125381-Reviews-Glendo_State_Park-
Glendo_Wyoming.html

Kids & youth - Olympic National Park (U.s. national Park service).
(n.d.). Nps.gov.
https://www.nps.gov/olym/learn/kidsyouth/index.htm

Mount St. Helens Visitor Center. (n.d.). Parks.wa.gov.
https://www.parks.wa.gov/245/Mount-St-Helens

Palouse Falls State Park heritage site. (n.d.). Parks.wa.gov.
https://www.parks.wa.gov/559/Palouse-Falls-State-Park-
Heritage-Site

Peglar, T. (2022, April 21). Where should I camp in Olympic
National Park? Olympic National Park Trips.
https://www.myolympicpark.com/where-to-stay-camp-
eat/camping-rv/where-should-i-camp-in-olympic/

Walnut, J. (2019, June 20). Camping at Deception Pass State Park in Washington. Beyond The Tent. https://www.beyondthetent.com/camping-deception-pass-state-park/

Washington state parks and recreation commission. (n.d.). Parks.wa.gov. https://www.parks.wa.gov/

(N.d.). Alltrails.com. https://www.alltrails.com/trail/us/washington/harrys-ridge?u=m

25 best North Carolina state & national parks. (n.d.). VacationIdea. https://vacationidea.com/north-carolina/best-north-carolina-parks.html

Hedinger, C. (2022, February 7). Carolina Beach State Park, NC (7 great things to do there!). NC Tripping. https://www.nctripping.com/carolina-beach-state-park/

Goose Creek: Camping. (n.d.). Ncparks.gov. https://www.ncparks.gov/state-parks/goose-creek-state-park/camping

4 best state parks in Montana for RV owners to visit. (2021, May 27). Bankston Motor Homes Blog. https://www.bankstonmotorhomes.com/blog/4-best-state-parks-in-montana-for-rv-owners-to-visit/

Bearmouth Chalet and camping on the river. (n.d.). Bearmouthchalet.com. http://www.bearmouthchalet.com/

Big Arm State Park. (n.d.). Visitmt.com.
https://www.visitmt.com/listings/general/state-park/big-
arm-state-park

Chalet Bearmouth RV Park. (n.d.). Visitmt.com.
https://www.visitmt.com/listings/general/private-
campground/chalet-bearmouth-rv-park

Columbia Falls RV Park. (n.d.). Columbiafallsrvpark.com.
https://www.columbiafallsrvpark.com/

Fees & general information. (n.d.). Fwp.mt.gov.
https://fwp.mt.gov/buyandapply/fees-and-general-
information

Lewis & Clark Caverns State Park. (n.d.). Outdoorsy.
https://www.outdoorsy.com/guide/lewis-clark-caverns-state-
park-mt

Montana. (2021, July 27). Togo RV. https://togorv.com/rvers-state-
park-campgrounds/montana/

Peglar, T. (2022, April 22). 8 RV tips for. Yellowstone National
Park. https://www.yellowstonepark.com/where-to-stay-
camp-eat/camping-rv-parks/rv-tips/

Salmon lake State Park. (n.d.). Fwp.mt.gov.
https://fwp.mt.gov/salmon-lake

The Lewis & Clark Caverns State Park trail system. (n.d.).
Fwp.mt.gov.
https://fwp.mt.gov/binaries/content/assets/fwp/stateparks/do
cuments/lccsp-trail-brochure-2021.pdf

Top 10 campgrounds & RV parks in Montana. (2022, May 12).
RVshare. https://rvshare.com/blog/top-10-
campgrounds/montana

Florida State Park rules. (n.d.). Florida State Parks.
https://www.floridastateparks.org/index.php/Rules

Rountree, B., & Gross, B. (2021, October 3). Best Florida state
parks: Our 8 favorites. Florida Rambler.
https://www.floridarambler.com/florida-parks-forests-
wildlife-refuges/best-florida-state-parks/

Sep. (2020, September 21). Florida state parks, preserves, rec areas,
and trails: Nearly 200 natural adventures. Visitflorida.com.
https://www.visitflorida.com/travel-ideas/articles/outdoors-
nature-florida-state-parks-natural-adventures/

Three Rivers State Park. (n.d.). Florida State Parks.
https://www.floridastateparks.org/parks-and-trails/three-
rivers-state-park

Always On Liberty. (2021, April 30). RV black tank cleaning and
maintenance tips. Always On Liberty.
https://alwaysonliberty.com/2021/04/rv-maintenance-how-
to-clean-your-rv-black-tank.html/

Buemi, M. (2018, August 19). A comprehensive guide to common
RV problems and how to solve them. RVshare.
https://rvshare.com/blog/rv-maintenance-problems/

Bungartz, A. (2020, June 8). Backing up and pulling through: How
to park your RV. Togo RV. https://togorv.com/rv-
living/how-to-park-rv/

How to park an RV. (n.d.). Reserveamerica.com.
https://www.reserveamerica.com/outdoors/how-to-park-an-
rv.htm

How To Properly Operate Your RV Propane Stove. (n.d.).
Lakeshore RV Center. https://lakeshore-rv.com/blog/how-
to-properly-operate-your-rv-propane-stove

Johnson, D. (2022, July 9). Leaving the Campground – part 6 of 7
in a series about traveling with an RV or travel trailer.
Tinytowable.com - All about Campgrounds and Small
Travel Trailers; tinyTowable.
https://tinytowable.com/leaving-the-campground-2/

Jon, T. (2021, August 17). How to turn on an electric water heater
in an RV (quick tutorial). Camper FAQs.
https://camperfaqs.com/how-to-turn-on-electric-water-
heater-in-rv

Jones, M. (2020, January 4). 10 RV maintenance mistakes to avoid.
Unique RV Camping with Harvest Hosts; Harvest Hosts.
https://harvesthosts.com/rv-camping/10-rv-maintenance-
mistakes-to-avoid/

Robichaud, D. (2015, April 15). Top 10 tips to successfully maintain your RV. Campersinn.com. https://blog.campersinn.com/blog/top-10-tips-to-successfully-maintain-your-rv

Milton Keynes UK
Ingram Content Group UK Ltd.
UKHW020632140923
428670UK00014B/724

9 781088 225189